D1449336

BOATBUILDING AND REPAIRING WITH FIBERGLASS

BOATBUILDING AND REPAIRING WITH FIBERGLASS

by Melvin D.C. Willis

INTERNATIONAL MARINE PUBLISHING COMPANY
CAMDEN, MAINE

© 1972 by International Marine Publishing Company
Library of Congress Catalog Card No. 74-176120
International Standard Book No. 0-87742-018-1
Printed in U.S.A.

Sixth Printing, 1983

Published by International Marine Publishing Company
21 Elm Street, Camden, Maine 04843
(207) 236-4342

*DEDICATED TO THE DREAMER WHO WANTS A BOAT
BUT CANNOT AFFORD ONE*

Contents

Preface

This book was originally published as the text for several 10-week-long (one evening a week) fiberglass technique courses I taught to members of the Oklahoma City Chapter of the International Amateur Boat Building Society. The club was largely the result of my own efforts during off-duty hours while I was in the Coast Guard assigned to the Coast Guard Institute in Oklahoma City.

Although the fiberglass division of the Oklahoma City Chapter closed with my departure for more nautical places (Maine), my experience indicates that it definitely is possible for a boatbuilding club to build fiberglass boats for one-third the retail cost. Of crucial importance is the choice of a boat which most members would want. Next most important would be to have the molded parts so designed that the assembly work would not be difficult. To make such a club work, unless a large space is available, the boats would have to be laid up quickly, and each finished at the individual club member's home.

Such boatbuilding activity is rewarding and fun. It is hoped that this book will increase the fun shared by boatbuilders by helping them avoid pitfalls, and that it will also increase their rewards in terms of better boats.

Melvin D. C. Willis

Thanks be unto

Bob Hakes, able founder of the Oklahoma City Chapter of IABBS, who suggested that I write a pamphlet on building fiberglass boats, which grew and grew and grew.

Henry Mertens, whose dedicated assistance helped me publish the first edition of this book and operate the Oklahoma City Chapter of IABBS.

Janice, good wife, who patiently tolerated my hiding myself away with this writing and the aforementioned club for months.

And others, particularly Blair Fletcher, of Fletcher Marine Products, Cherry Hill, N. J., in whose employ I first became interested in fiberglass.

BOATBUILDING
AND REPAIRING
WITH FIBERGLASS

INTRODUCTION

A fiberglass hull is a thin (1/8″ to 1/4″) shell usually composed of two distinct layers: outermost is a thin (1/64″) layer of colored, hard, shiny resin which gives a bright finish; inside of the first layer, and bonded to it, is one or more layers of fiberglass cloth saturated with polyester resin. The cloth is made of flexible but strong glass strands; the resin is rigid (when cured) but not strong. Resin plus fiberglass cloth results in a rigid, strong reinforcement for the thin, fragile, but hard and shiny, outer layer. The overall composite shell is watertight, rot-proof, insect-proof, and fairly easy to keep clean. Designed properly, fiberglass construction can be as strong as conventional wood construction.

WHY FIBERGLASS?

What is all the excitement about fiberglass? Is it really as good as, or better than, other boatbuilding materials? The tests conducted on three Coast Guard patrol boats provide an answer: "A Report on Long Term Durability of Fiberglass Boats," appearing in *Yachting* (September, 1962), reveals that fiberglass is a superior material for marine use.

The Coast Guard built many 40-foot patrol boats in the early 1950s. Most of them were of steel construction. But for experimental purposes, three were built of fiberglass. In 1962, after 10 years of use, these three were thoroughly cleaned and examined for deterioration; additionally, three foot-square panels were cut out of their hulls, decks, and cabin tops for extensive laboratory analyses.

These patrol boats measure 40′3″ overall, with a beam of 11′3″, and weigh in at 21,000 pounds displacement. Powered by twin 250 hp diesels, they can make a top speed of 22 knots.

Routine service reports indicated the three fiberglass boats had stood up well, incurring only one fifth the maintenance costs of the steel models.

Each had had long hours of service in both salt and fresh water. The oldest one had been delivered in April of 1952, had 7,600 hours of service, first in the Chesapeake Bay, then in Virginia, and later in Texas. At the time of the study, all three were operating out of Houston in the Houston Ship Canal. They had been especially chosen for that duty because wastes dumped in the canal from oil and gas refineries had resulted in a high concentration of sulphuric acid, which was extremely destructive to the steel boats that served there previously. Although one of the fiberglass boats had been there for eight years, it showed no ill effects. The inspection showed the hull and deck laminates to be in excellent condition. There were no dents, distortion, or decomposition.

The panels which were cut out looked as if they had just been laid up. The edges showed no penetration of the oil and dirt that had accumulated in the bilges.

An interesting note is that one of the three fiberglass boats had served next to a steel-hull version on one occasion while trying to combat a fire on an oil tanker. The fiberglass boat had been able to operate closer to the intense heat of the flames than the steel one because of the low heat conductivity of fiberglass. Although the paint was scorched (the boats were painted to maintain their fresh appearance, as were the steel ones), the laminate did not ignite, nor was it otherwise damaged. And note this: these boats were *not* molded of fire-retardant resin, which now is available but was not when these boats were built.

So what is all the excitement about? You mean all this started from a discovery made by a man in 1909 looking for a material to stiffen shirt collars?

The Navy had its first fiberglass boats as early as 1946, about which time a few outboard runabouts and sailboats were first being made of fiberglass. By the 1960s, fiberglass boats had edged their way into the majority at the boat shows. Now it is hard to find a boat made of anything else at a boat show. Large sailboats are vastly outnumbered by motorboats, but, starting with just one manufacturer of fiberglass auxiliaries in 1959, there are now over 80 manufacturers of fiberglass auxiliaries (not counting manufacturers of little sailboats with no auxiliary power). Almost every new sailboat coming out on the market today is made of fiberglass.

That is what the excitement is all about!

CAN THE AMATEUR SAVE MONEY?

The International Amateur Boat Building Society (IABBS), which sponsored this book, advertises "build your own boat for one third the cost." Can you, as an amateur, starting from scratch, build a fiberglass boat using the techniques described in this book, and save two thirds of the retail cost of the boat of your choice?

Some time ago, I analyzed the cost of producing a 16' fiberglass canoe. The results of that study will help answer these questions. If you want to build just one 16' fiberglass canoe, and can find someone to loan you his new canoe just long enough to make a mold from it, although it would take you only 17 hours of actual work, it would cost you at least $240 to make the mold and then one canoe from that mold. On the other hand, if a small fiberglass boatbuilding business, which was already producing boats, wanted to do the same thing (perhaps as a prototype), it would cost only $150 in materials because of the discounts available to quantity buyers.

Such a canoe can be bought for around $200, however, so it would not pay you to try to build just one boat using the techniques described in this book. The primary reason for this is that you would be discarding the expensive mold which would still be good for at least another 24 canoes. It would pay the boatbuilder to build the canoe.

But suppose you decided to make a few more canoes to sell, keeping one of them for yourself. Now the story changes radically. If you bought the materials in large enough quantities to build one mold and 25 canoes, it would cost you only $50 per canoe for materials. It would involve an initial investment of around $1,225 and about 400 hours of work, but you could pay for the entire cost of materials and reimburse yourself about $1.14 an hour if you sold the 24 extra canoes for $70 each. At that price, well beneath the usual retail price of $200, you should have no trouble selling them. When you were done, you could throw the mold away, keep the best canoe for yourself, and be about $455 richer. If you managed to sell the 24 boats at the full retail price ($200), you would receive about $3,600 for them.

Perhaps you would like to know what similar figures would be for a small fiberglass sailboat, such as a sailboard. If you build a sailboard mold and then only one boat from it, the venture would cost you about $396, with actual working time of 31 hours (this does not include setting-up, clean-up, and break time). If a factory did the same thing, materials would cost about $245. The boat retails new for about $400. But in batches of 25 per each mold, each boat would cost only $200 to build (price includes $2.00/hour for labor), with a profit of $200 per boat, or $5,000 for the 25 completed boats.

The techniques described in this book are the ones actually being used in about 400 companies throughout the United States. The question you are probably asking yourself is: Is fiberglass boatbuilding a good line of business for the small businessman with limited capital, or for the man who wants a side business in addition to his regular job? Other builder's experiences should help answer this question.

FIBERGLASS BOATBUILDING — A GOOD BUSINESS?

Let us take a look at what is beginning to happen in the fiberglass industry. You can learn an important lesson from "A Boat Every Two Minutes," an article that appeared in the September/October 1965 issue of *Reinforced Plastics*, which described the new Traveler Boat plant. The $6 million plant contained 370,000 square feet of production area. Its materials-handling systems, purchasing, payroll, etc., were handled by an IBM 1440 computer. The layout of the plant was designed for efficient production of their product — motorboats, one of which they could turn out every two minutes (it took only four hours to build one from start to final inspection). If they geared the plant to full three-shift production, the plant could turn out enough boats in one year to match the industry's entire 1964 production.

The plant was located in Danville, Illinois, 150 miles from the population center of the U. S. (Salem, Ill.). Traveler had closed its other plants in New York, California, Wisconsin, and Arkansas, in order to consolidate their operation in one centrally located, highly efficient plant. Special railroad cars were built to hold 24 boats each, which were more economical and safer than trucks for delivery to boat dealers and strategically located warehouses throughout the United States.

What does this say for the small businessman contemplating fiberglass boatbuilding? Does it mean the small boatbuilder will soon be an anachronism, unable to survive economically with the competition from the giants?

At present no one firm dominates the market. The top eight manufacturers account for less than 30% of the market, out of about 400 firms which manufacture fiberglass boats of all sizes. However the trend is clear — the boat industry is going to more and more resemble the auto industry, and this will spell the doom of many small builders. This growth, making boatbuilding one of the 10 largest industries in the nation, is being spurred by the rapid increase in recreational boating. Since 1908, when there were only some 100,000 pleasure boats, boating has grown dramatically. There are over 8,000,000 pleasure boats, and over 40,000,000 people use these boats (one out of every five Americans).* In its report to Congress, the Outdoor Recreation Resources Review Commission predicted a 317% increase in recreational boating over the next 40 years.

The small firm must seek its business in boats for which there is less demand. Big firms present competition that is too strong for motorboats

---

*See "A 60-Year Survey of the Sport of Boating" in the February 1968 issue of *Motor Boating*.

in the 10- to 25-foot market. Although not presently the case, it is conceivable that mass production methods will soon be introduced in the manufacture of certain sailboats; we have seen the rapid growth of such sailboats as the *Sunfish* and the *Sailfish,* which portend this development.

The small firm can make a profit from the construction of luxury yachts, workboats, and the many sailboats of smaller classes. Excluding the biggest sailboat classes, there are approximately 375 classes of distinctive sailboats in the world with an average of 650 boats in each class. This is the result of many years' growth. This is (on a yearly basis) much too small a market to make mass-production methods feasible. And this diversity of sailboat classes is well entrenched in sailing circles, because each class has special characteristics which their owners are proud of. Because of the character of people who sail, it is safe to predict that sailing will not soon be reduced to a few standardized, mass-produced classes, and perhaps never. Catering to these tastes will continue to be the haven for the small-time boat builder.

WHAT ABOUT THE BOAT REPAIR BUSINESS?

If you study the trends of business in this country, you will see two parallel developments. As manufacturing industries tend toward bigness and mass-production, there has been a tremendous growth of small, service enterprises. Every growing community has a welter of small businesses which clean, repair, or alter what you buy from the giants. With the ever-increasing growth of boating, there is going to be a corresponding growth of the need for reputable and efficient boat and engine repair facilities, and also winter storage facilities. Even though it is possible to learn how to repair fiberglass boats, with a subsequent savings in repair bills, there are a great many people who still will not want to be bothered with doing such work. Because boat repairing is not a luxury but a necessity to the boatowner in trouble, the fiberglass repair business is lucrative. Repair work, in addition to the construction of low-demand specialty yachts during slack periods, will keep the small boatbuilder solidly in the black.

WHAT ABOUT THE AMATEUR REPAIRER?

If you are one of those hardy boatowners who is not bothered by the thought of doing your own repairs, Chapter 5, on making fiberglass repairs, will repay the price of this book many times if you have to make just one repair on the hull or deck of your boat during the years you own it. Many repair situations are discussed in detail, with an abundance of drawings. By reading the rest of the book you will understand how fiberglass boats are made, and the "why" behind the "how" of repair procedures.

Though an individual can not make just one fiberglass boat from scratch economically, he can make just one repair economically, because in repairs little material is involved. The skill of the workers and the overhead involved in maintaining repairmen on call all the time are the real expenses in all repair work. Both of these you can supply yourself if you choose to study how.

Also, if you are a wary buyer, reading this book will help you know what is going on when you purchase a boat. Chapter 2, "Making the Small Fiberglass Boat," discusses the problems fiberglass construction can give the builder, and ultimately the user, if the work is not done carefully.

THE INTERNATIONAL AMATEUR BOAT BUILDING SOCIETY

In the last couple of years we have seen rise on the national scene a new force, or at least a force newly vocal — consumer pressure groups. The International Amateur Boat Building Society is a consumer group that has recently been formed to (among other things) try to "beat" the prices of everything marine. Everything in recreational boating seems to be priced high above what almost identical items for a nonboating use are priced. IABBS offers its members substantial discounts on most marine items. Write to IABBS, 3183 Merrill, Royal Oak, Mich. 48072, for more information.

The primary and original purpose of writing this book was to supplement a course in fiberglass hand-layup boatbuilding. As the IABBS building centers located in various cities throughout the United States (and soon the world) become more fully organized, they may have a variety of molds for various fiberglass boats which members can use to make themselves professional-quality boats at substantial savings.

By having molds available to members free of charge, members could have boats at a large savings. Furthermore, to support itself, the local chapter could manufacture an occassional boat to sell at a reduced price to someone who could not get a boat otherwise. These activities are not intended as a threat, or unfair competition, to established boatbuilders who must make a profit to survive: the people obtaining boats this way would in all probability not be boatowners at all otherwise. And there will always be an overwhelmingly large number of people who would not built or repair their own boats even if the tools and materials were handed to them on a gold platter: after all, no matter how simplified it may be made for them, it still is work.

JUST HOW MUCH WORK IS IT?

Perhaps you were startled by the 17 hours total construction time given for the canoe mold and the one completed canoe from it. Naturally, as a beginner, you couldn't do the job in 17 hours. First of all, the 17 hours does not include all the time lost "in motion," that is, setting things up, thinking about the job, cleaning up, taking breaks, interruptions, etc. But just as important, you would not know exactly what you were doing, and therefore would be slow and make mistakes that would have to be corrected. But an experienced worker could surely do the job in double the time, loafing along half the time, breaks included, etc. (Actually an experienced worker working conscientiously should be able to do the job in close to the 17 hours given.) If you are fortunate enough to be near an IABBS center where a course in fiberglass is being conducted, you will actually get to do some fiberglass work and should quickly pick up a good deal of skill.

There is something about fiberglass that keeps you from being slow — namely the penalty of being slow! The resins you use are like a time-bomb that can not be changed once activated: you either work fast and efficiently or you loose your money that is tied up in the materials. In fiberglass work, labor is cheap and materials are expensive.

DEMISE OF TRAVELER BOAT WORKS

Even the mass production of fiberglass boats using the most advanced techniques available can founder without experienced labor and careful quality control. The Traveler Boats plant at Danville, Illinois, went out of business and was the scene of a big auction in November, 1967. Molds for 14- and 16-foot outboard boats sold for between $400 and $800 a set. I have gathered from hearsay that the plant suffered from a severe shortage of trained labor: on occasion, as much as one-half of a day's production had to be destroyed because of gross defects caused by worker error. Although it is interesting that this mammoth plant did not survive, I do not think its demise changes my contention that companies producing the most popular lines of boats are going over to mass production. In my opinion, the fall of Traveler Boats does show that quality can make the difference between success and failure for the amateur builder, the small builder, or the large builder.

1/ MATERIALS and TOOLS

Fiberglass boats are not really all fiberglass—they are made of layers of various types of fiberglass impregnated with resin, which makes up a large part of the composition of the boat. The outside layer is a thin layer of pure resin called gel coat. Molded within the layers of fiberglass and resin are sometimes layers of balsa wood, plywood, or foam; and attached to the inside of fiberglass boats, out of view, are usually several small pieces of wood which serve as back-ups for fittings.

A fiberglass boat is made in an open cavity mold. Perhaps you have seen gelatin made in a mold which is "inside-out" — that is, the outside of the molded gelatin takes the shape of the inside of the mold. In a similar way, a fiberglass boat is molded in an "inside-out" mold which has its smooth side inside, so that the outside of the boat made in it will be smooth.

However, unlike molded gelatin, a fiberglass boat is not poured. First, after waxing the mold so the boat will not stick, a layer of special, colored resin (gel coat) is sprayed in — this will be the shiny outside of the boat when done. Then layer after layer of fiberglass is fitted into the mold and saturated with resin, which a little later hardens. The fiberglass gives the boat its strength, and the resin after it has hardened holds the boat in shape. Wood or foam, if it is to be added, goes between layers of fiberglass and resin so that there is fiberglass evenly on both sides. Wood backup blocks are attached after the last layer is on. When the resin in all the layers has finally hardened enough, the boat is pulled out of the mold, allowing the mold to be used for additional boats.

The above process is described in great detail in Chapter 2, where all the steps needed to build a 14′ sailboard are traced. This chapter lists and briefly describes everything required to build a 14′ sailboard and also all that is needed to make the plug and molds described in Chapter 3. In addition there are some other items which are not used in this particular boat, but which occur frequently enough in fiberglass work to be included — such items are marked with an asterisk (*) in the list of materials below.

Not everything is discussed in much detail, and some items are listed but not discussed at all, because they are common to the boating scene (like varnish and rope) and not peculiar to fiberglass construction. They have been included to make the list complete and to illustrate what a large number of items is required to construct a relatively simple boat like our example.

You will notice that molds and patterns are listed first as items which you already have. And then, looking ahead to Chapters 2 and 3, you will notice that building the fiberglass boat is discussed before building the molds.

There are three reasons for this seemingly reversed order. First, the book was written primarily for those who have access to molds, as the process described is not economical for a person who wants to build just one boat.

Second, and more important, the basics in handling fiberglass are identical for building the boat and the mold. If you know how to build the boat, you will know how to do all the fiberglass work required on the mold — therefore Chapter 3 discusses in detail all the steps leading up to the fiberglass work in building the mold.

Third, it is more useful to discuss fiberglass-handling procedures in relation to the boat than to the mold. Some readers will want only to learn how fiberglass boats are built, so they can be more knowledgeable when surveying boats for purchase, or to help them understand repair procedures.

LIST OF MATERIALS
MOLDS
Hull
Deck
Cockpit
Daggerboard trunk

PATTERNS
Daggerboard
Rudder
*Hull reinforcement
*Deck reinforcement
*Cockpit reinforcement

FIBERGLASS MATERIALS
Matt cloth
Woven cloth

Roving (heavy woven cloth)
"Fabmat" (matt and roving combination)

RESINS
Gel coat, color of boat
Black gel coat
Polyester resin
Activator (MEK peroxide)
*Cobalt napthanate (accelerator)
Thick epoxy resin (consistency of putty)

SOLVENTS
Acetone
Styrene

MOLD MATERIALS
Wax
Release agent
Tacky cloth
Buffing compounds

TOOLS AND EQUIPMENT
Spray gun and compressor
Power drill and bits
Sander and sandpaper
Buffer
Exhaust fan
Fire extinguisher(s)
Hand truck (for moving barrels of resin)
Barrel stand (to hold barrel horizontally)
Seacock-type spigot for barrel
Rack to hold rolls of fiberglass
Squeeze bottles to hold activator
Measuring cups (1-oz. medicine)
*Meter-dispenser (to fit activator gallon jug)
Roller (for removing air bubbles)
*Radius roller (for corners)
Squeegee
Scissors
Sharp knife
Brushes, narrow and wide (unpainted handles)
Pails, old coffee cans, or paper tubs
Rags
Face mask

Respirator
Rubber gloves
Barrier cream

CORES — STIFFENERS
*Wood strips
*Mailing tubes
*Plywood
*Foam sheets
*Balsa panels
*Honeycomb paper

BACKUPS (for hardware)
Wood (short lengths of plank)

ASSEMBLING MATERIALS
Pop-rivets
Plastic tubing (for mast tube)
Rubber molding (rub rail hides assembly joint)
Liquid ready-to-mix foam

MISCELLANEOUS ITEMS
Bow handle
Drain plug
Mast
Boom
Sail(s)
Foam flotation (solid plank and liquid)
Rudder and tiller fittings
Traveler rod or wire
Several blocks
Line
Various marine hardware
Screws, other fastenings
Mahogany and plywood to make:
    tiller
    daggerboard
    rudder
    splash shield
    other trim

MOLD AND PLUG-MAKING MATERIALS
Plaster
Screening

Rough plywood
Other rough lumber
Staples, fastenings
Long battens
Tooling gel coat

PRICES

Specific prices are always of interest. Usually they are not included in a book of this type because they cannot be made applicable to all locations and are impossible to keep current. However, unlike the businessman, the amateur builder does not have the facilities and means to make meaningful cost analyses before engaging in a project. Therefore specific prices have been included as a guide, to give you an idea of the economics of this construction method. Before committing yourself to an expensive project, however, protect yourself by obtaining current prices.

Prices are quoted primarily for fiberglass materials only. Most of the prices are broken down into the following three categories:

1. Price of material when bought in small quantities in retail stores.

2. Price of material when bought by mail (usually small quantities) from a company specializing in fiberglass supplies such as Defender Industries, 384 Broadway, New York, New York 10013 (catalog is $0.75). There are other companies selling fiberglass supplies through the mails, the names of which can be obtained through ads in boating magazines and in *Amateur Boat Building*, the official IABBS publication. The reason why I quote so many prices from Defender Industries in this book is because I have had so much experience with them. This does not mean however, that I favor or recommend them over all others. You will undoubtedly find many catalog sales companies that will provide good products and good service.

3. Price of material when bought in the smallest quantities available from industrial suppliers (the smallest quantities usually are quite large from the point of view of amateur builders). Furthermore, prices will be broken down to give an idea of the overall costs of the project.

The prices being quoted are typical of those prevailing in 1970, and should be adjusted for yearly inflation. In the case of purchasing from a mail-order house, most of the items cannot go parcel post because either they are too large and heavy or they are flammable liquids, which are barred from the mails. Therefore they will probably be sent by truck, which costs about $10.00 per hundred pounds from New York to Oklahoma City, for example.

When you are considering purchasing large quantities of materials from an industrial supplier, you must consider the shelf life of the items.

Many resins will not be good if kept for more than six months, others as low as three months, depending on the conditions of storage and how old the product was when you received it. Such considerations might make it better to order smaller quantities from a mail-order house at a somewhat higher price.

GEL COAT RESIN

Fiberglass boats are built in layers. The outermost layer, the one you see when the boat is finished, is made of a special, opaque resin which has been specially formulated to make it scratch resistant. This outermost layer, called the *gel coat* by most manufacturers, is sprayed into the mold in an even layer about 15 to 20 mils thick (a mil is a thousandth of an inch, making 15 mils about 1/64 of an inch).

Gel coat comes from the manufacturer as a thick liquid. Just before spraying it into the mold, a small amount of a clear liquid, called *activator* or *catalyst,* is stirred in thoroughly. The catalyst causes a chemical reaction to take place which causes all the gel-coat molecules to link together and form a solid material in a matter of a few minutes. The speed with which the liquid turns solid depends on the amount of catalyst added and the temperature (the more catalyst and the higher the temperature, the faster the cure, or setting up).

PRICE OF GEL COAT RESIN

Gel coat is not always available at retail marine stores. However, such stores often sell tubes of solid pigment which can be stirred into regular laminating resin. Prices vary greatly but probably average somewhere around $16.00 per gallon. (Actually the amounts sold are much smaller than gallons.)

Because amateur builders so seldom use gel coat, a place like Defender Industries carries only clear gel coat to which you must add a color concentrate, which is sold in several colors. The cost of the two is about $10.00 per gallon, plus shipping.

Industrial suppliers normally will not sell gel coat by the gallon. The smallest size available is a five-gallon pail, a lot of gel coat for an amateur. The price varies according to the color, but ranges between $35.00 and $50.00 per five-gallon pail. Black and white are usually the cheapest: a pretty bright red might cost almost $50.00 for five gallons.

GEL COAT RESIN USED IN A TYPICAL BOAT

To give you an idea of the amount of gel coat you would need for a typical project, let us suppose you are going to make a mold for the sailboard discussed in Chapter 2, and then make a boat out of it for yourself. You will probably want to make the boat in two colors, say a white hull and blue deck. The molds will be black, and you will use black behind the white or blue as discussed in Chapter 2.

Including inevitable wastage, you will probably use three gallons of black gel coat to make the molds, and another gallon to make the boat. It will certainly be worthwhile to buy a five-gallon pail of black. But you probably will use only 1½ gallons of white and one gallon of blue. It will be cheaper to buy these colors by the gallon, unless you plan to use the molds to build more boats to sell.

If you should go into manufacturing in a big way, the price will fall rapidly as you buy gel coat in large quantities. The real price break comes when you buy it by the drum (55 gallons). When bought by the drum, gel coat is priced at so many cents per pound. A typical price of white gel coat bought by the drum might be $0.50 per pound. Since there is from 500 to 520 pounds per drum, the price will be about $280 per drum, which works out to be $5.10 per gallon, a considerable saving over buying it by the five-gallon pail.

PRICE AND WEIGHT PER SQUARE FOOT

The approximate cost per square foot of white gel coat applied 20 mils thick, including catalyst, solvents, mold release, and allowance for waste, is $0.18, when purchased in single-drum quantities. The approximate weight per square foot of the same gel coat is two ounces.

TOOLING GEL COAT

Tooling gel coat is a special gel coat for use on molds where extra toughness is required. It is more brittle than regular gel coat, which itself is more brittle than regular laminating resin (to get toughness and scratch resistance you have to accept brittleness). Usually only black or orange is used, for reasons explained in Chapter 3.

In practice many small shops use black gel coat for their molds instead of black tooling gel coat as there is little difference between them. Tooling gel coat costs about $8.00 per gallon in five-gallon lots.

POLYESTER RESIN

After the gel coat has cured, it must be reinforced with one or more layers of fiberglass plus plastic resin. The fiberglass is laid on the gel coat, and resin is brushed on the fiberglass. Just prior to brushing on the resin, activator must be added in the proper amount and stirred in. Like the gel coat, the resin will soon become solid. The fiberglass gives the boat strength, and the resin, after it cures, holds the fiberglass in the desired shape.

CHARACTERISTICS OF POLYESTER RESIN

There are many kinds of resin. The kind that is used primarily with the hand-layup process described in this book is a "low viscosity, prepromoted, thixotropic, room-temperature-curing polyester resin." *Prepromoted* means that all the chemicals required for it to cure have already been added, except for activator which you add just prior to use. *Low viscosity* means watery or thin, making it easy to spray and wet out (saturate) fiberglass. *Thixotropic* means you get a minimum of runs or sags when the resin is applied to a vertical surface. Some resins cure only at high temperatures: the kind used by most laminators will cure readily at 70° F. or above. *Polyester* is the type of plastic; epoxy resins are also used for some applications that require extra adhesion, but because of their higher cost, are not used for most fiberglass construction.

DIFFERENCES AMONG BOAT RESINS

Low viscosity and thixotrophy must be balanced against each other. It should be obvious that a resin cannot be both thin and run-free. Resins are compounded to give a good compromise of these characteristics. Some manufacturers offer resins which have more of one quality at the sacrifice of the other.

There are some differences in the quality of resin. The more expensive resins usually have more desirable handling and strength characteristics. When purchasing resins, especially from a dealer whose reputation is not established, you must be careful that what you are getting is of boatbuilding quality, as there are resins put out for industrial applications that do not meet boatbuilding standards.

The primary difference among resins is whether a wax solution has been added or not. Resin which does not have a wax solution will dry "tacky." This is because it is *air-inhibited,* meaning that air prevents the outside surface from curing. The surface of such a resin will remain sticky even though the rest has hardened after the activator has been added. However, if a wax solution is also added, during application the wax will float to the surface and cut off the air. The resin will then cure hard throughout, including the surface. Although this would seem desirable, actually the type that cures tacky is much to be preferred, for reasons that will be discussed in Chapter 2.

Also some resins are *fire-retardant.* This quality is obtained by an additive which can be purchased separately and mixed in, or you can buy the resin with it already added. Fire retardant resin will not ignite as easily as ordinary resin. Also once set afire, when the flame is removed, it will eventually extinguish itself, whereas regular resin will continue burning rapidly. However, fire-retardant resin is seldom used in fiberglass construction because of its high cost, and because it sometimes causes fabrication problems.

PRICES OF BOAT RESIN

Retail stores sell polyester resin by the quart and gallon, with the necessary activator included in the price. Typical prices are $8.00 to $11.00 per gallon.

Defender Industries sells several grades of resin. Its regular grade sells for $5.10 per gallon. The price drops to $4.80 per gallon if you buy five gallons, and $3.00 per gallon if you buy a 55-gallon drum (but activator is not included in the drum size). As a comparison, their fire-retardant resin costs $9.70 per gallon, $9.10 per gallon in five-gallon lots, and $7.95 per gallon in 25-gallon lots (55-gallon drum size not quoted).

Industrial suppliers will seldom supply less than one 55-gallon drum. Activator is never included and must be bought separately. They price it by the pound, and most drums contain 500 pounds of resin (resin weighs about 9.3 pounds per gallon). A typical price is from $0.23 to $0.25 per pound, which makes it about $118 to $125 per drum. Incidentally, the weight of drums sometimes varies according to how full they are: a drum might weigh as much as 525 pounds. As a comparison, a typical price of fire-retardant resin is $0.36 per pound, which makes it $180 per drum. The per-gallon price works out to be about $2.15 for regular resin, versus $3.30 for fire-retardant resin. If you buy five or more drums at one time you can save several dollars per drum.

COST OF RESIN IN A TYPICAL BOAT

Since resin is combined with fiberglass, there are no layers of just resin alone. The amount of resin soaked by the fiberglass varies according to the type of fiberglass used. We will discuss this in detail later. Suffice it to say for now that a fiberglass boat can be from 50% to 75% resin by weight, so that of the $75 or so that it might cost to build the bare hull, deck, and cockpit of the sailboard discussed in Chapter 2, about $20 is in gel coat resin, and about $30 is in laminating resin.

ACTIVATOR

Polyester resin requires a promoter and an activator or catalyst to cure. Most resins you will buy for hand-layup fiberglass work will be prepromoted, requiring only the addition of activator to initiate the cure. The term *activator* has been used throughout this text for what many manufacturers call *catalyst*. The chemical name for activator is MEK *peroxide*.

In quantities up to a 55-gallon drum, polyester resin usually has the necessary amount of activator included in its price. However gel coat usually does not have the activator included in its price in quantities as small as a five-gallon pail.

Defender Industries charges almost $18.00 for one gallon of activator. The price from an industrial supplier for a single gallon varies from $13.00 to $20.00. However, if four gallons are bought at once, the price drops to between $9.60 and $13.00 per gallon. Actually the price is quoted as so much per pound, and it so happens that a gallon weighs exactly eight pounds, and that, very conveniently, one fluid ounce weighs exactly one weight-type ounce.

As discussed later, on the average you will use around one ounce of activator per gallon of resin. Since there are 55 gallons in a drum of resin, and 64 ounces in one-half gallon of activator, you will use approximately one-half gallon of activator for each drum of resin. Therefore you must add from $5.00 to $10.00 (according to the price you get) to the cost of resin when bought by the drum.

There are more concentrated MEK peroxides available from some suppliers which give more rapid cures for a similar amount used, but they are no more expensive to buy. Although you could save money by using these, the total cost of activator is small in comparison to the other materials which go into a fiberglass boat, and the extra difficulty of handling the very small quantities a stronger activator would involve is not worth the small amount you would save. As it is, the least potent activator involves volumes that are small enough to create a fair chance of error in measuring them out under working conditions.

DISPENSERS FOR ACTIVATOR

An inexpensive system for measuring out activator is to buy a small polyethylene squeeze bottle (available from suppliers for about $0.60 each), and buy paper or polyethylene one-ounce medicine cups from a hospital supply house which have markings on them for the various portions of an ounce. Measure out the amount of activator you need by squeezing it out into the medicine cup.

If you are doing a lot of fiberglassing, a safer and more convenient way is to buy a catalyst dispenser. It is a little pump made of non-corroding materials that screws into a gallon bottle of activator. It has an adjustable meter which gives exactly the amount of activator you want each time you use it. Unfortunately, the dispenser costs from $50.00 to $60.00.

MEK peroxide is very hazardous to use, causing bad burns if spilled on the skin and especially if splashed in the eyes. Immediate flushing of the skin or eyes with large quantities of water is required, and medical attention is necessary if the eyes are involved. It is best to wear a face mask when working with activator, as you never know when you might slip or something else might happen to cause some of it to be splashed in your eyes.

COBALT ACCELERATOR

Cobalt accelerator (the chemical name is cobalt napthanate) is a purple liquid used to greatly accelerate the cure of polyester resin. Only a few drops are needed.

Cobalt napthanate is hazardous to use, and normally there should never be any need for it. It is useful only in unusual situations when you have a small job which must be hurried, or when it is very cold (between 40 and 55° F.) and when it must be used for the resin to cure.

Always mix in activator thoroughly before adding cobalt napthanate to resin. Never add it directly to the activator, because it will react violently, possibly starting a fire.

The rapid cure caused by cobalt napthanate generates an excessive amount of heat and is to be avoided as a regular procedure as it may damage surrounding materials (particularly the gloss of the mold, even though it is protected by two or three layers of cloth which have already been put down). For most purposes you can obtain a faster cure by adding extra activator, or by exposing the part being worked on to a heat lamp or to the direct rays of the sun.

PRICE OF COBALT ACCELERATOR

Defender Industries sells cobalt napthanate under the name of "promoting agent;" enough for one gallon of resin costs $0.75. It is priced around $7.50 per gallon from industrial suppliers, enough for many, many gallons.

STYRENE

Just as turpentine is the thinner for many house paints, styrene is the thinner for resin and gel coat. Sometimes you have a need to thin the gel coat somewhat for sprayability, and some manufacturers use it to thin out the gel coat so that it will spread further. Styrene is at least as hazardous to handle as activator, and you must take all precautions against having it splash in your eyes (it is well to wear a mask when using it). Do not allow styrene to drop on a mold as it will soften the hardened resin and leave a mark.

From industrial suppliers, styrene is $7.00 per five-gallon pail. You can easily see the savings you can get by diluting the resin (however you should use no more than 5% styrene by volume in order to maintain resin quality). Styrene is not available from other sources of supply.

ACETONE

Acetone is a solvent which will dissolve polyester resin *before* it has cured. It is used to clean your tools and your hands or gloves. It is also harsh on your hands and eyes, but not nearly as much so as styrene and activator. It is extremely flammable. Do not drop it on a mold as it may leave a mark. Because acetone dissolves water, it is sometimes useful for cleaning traces of water from objects, after which it evaporates rapidly.

PRICE OF ACETONE

Sometimes you can find acetone in retail stores for $2.50 or more a gallon. A gallon costs $2.50 from Defender Industries. Bought from industrial suppliers, it will cost from $6.00 to $10.00 for a five-gallon pail, and from $50.00 to $90.00 for a 55-gallon drum. Being a more or less common chemical, acetone is available from a number of chemical suppliers as well as suppliers of fiberglass materials.

CLEAR CASTING RESIN

For some special purposes, you may require a polyester resin that is perfectly clear when it cures, rather than the greenish-brown that most resins turn when cured. The most typical use of such a resin is for fiberglassing a surfboard so that the wood core can show through, or for other such decorative uses. Although milky when first activated, clear casting resin turns a beautiful water-like clear.

PRICE OF CLEAR CASTING RESIN

Defender Industries sells clear casting resin for $9.95 per gallon. A five-gallon pail costs about $24.00 from an industrial suppplier.

THICKENER

Various powders are available which you can add to resin to thicken it so that it becomes a paste. Whenever you have a large void to fill, this is one method of handling the situation.

Defender Industries sells phenolic microballoons—microscopic hollow balloons made of a petroleum product—for $10.50 for five pounds, which, because it is a lightweight material, is a sizable amount. Their steel powder costs $0.90 per pound; their thixotropic powder (also called cabosil) costs $0.90 per half pound. From industrial suppliers, cabosil costs about $12.00 for 10 pounds; talc about $10.00 for 50 pounds.

Also, you can use scraps of matt to thicken resin if you shred the matt. For some applications matt would be a better thickener and does not cost anything as you salvage it from scraps. If the application allows it, you can use sawdust, or the dust thrown off when grinding fiberglass.

When you add the powder to the resin, you probably will find that the resin sets up much faster than it would have otherwise. Therefore add less activator than usual when using a thickener. Mix in the activator before adding the powder as it will be difficult to mix the activator in thoroughly after you have made the paste.

TYPES OF REINFORCEMENT

After the gel coat is sprayed in the mold, it must be reinforced by one or more layers of fiberglass saturated with resin. There are a number of different kinds of fiberglass, and there are also other kinds of reinforcement that are not fiberglass at all. Briefly, they are:

Most-used reinforcements
    Matt (a nonwoven, felt-like cloth)
    Woven cloth (looks much like clothing cloth)
    Woven roving (a coarse open-weave cloth)
    "Fabmat" (combination of matt and roving)

Nonfiberglass reinforcements
    Dynel
    Vectra
    Stainless steel (still in development stage)

Dynel and Vectra are used primarily for covering wood boats, and are superior for this purpose to fiberglass woven cloth, which has been the standard for this operation. Some boat manufacturers are developing a cloth made of strands of stainless steel which will be superior to fiberglass because it will be stronger and lighter, and will provide an automatic built-in radar reflector, lightning protection, and a ground for electronics equipment.

Despite the above, fiberglass has proven to have great strength and versatility and presently is used as the reinforcement for plastic boats.

There is a great difference among the types of fiberglass available, which will be discussed in detail on the following pages.

Warning — all fiberglass cloths intended for boatbuilding must be specially treated at the end of the manufacturing process to remove oils used in their manufacture. The treatment is called *chroming* or *Volan Finish 114* (by Owens-Corning). In use the various fabrics are a chrome color before the application of resin, but turn translucent when saturated with resin and thus appear the color of the objects they cover.

For some industrial purposes, fiberglass does not have to be chromed. Some boatbuilders buy this unchromed cloth, which is less expensive, thinking they have a bargain, only their boats may fall apart as the resin will not bond properly with unchromed cloth. So be careful about bargains; make sure what you get is manufactured specifically for boatbuilding purposes.

FIBERGLASS MATT

Matt, spelled mat by many distributors, is composed of long (one to two inches in length) glass fibers randomly criss-crossed and interlocked. It is not a woven cloth and can be pulled apart, since it is held together by dried, unactivated resin which only sets up when wetted by activated resin. It is highly absorbent and should only be used when you must adhere a layer of fiberglass tightly to a sharply curved surface. It is also used between layers of woven cloth, between layers or roving, or as a waterproof layer when there is no gel coat to insure watertightness.

WOVEN CLOTH

Woven cloth is what most people visualize when fiberglass cloth is mentioned. Cloth is quite different from matt, as will be discussed later.* It is composed of small bundles of twisted strands of fiberglass tightly woven at right angles to each other. Usually it has a selvaged edge, that is, an edge that has been woven in such a manner that it will not unravel.

FIBERGLASS TAPE

Fiberglass tape is woven cloth manufactured in very narrow widths, intended for use on joints of wood boats and in a few other special applications. This is the product most boat and marine supply stores have if they carry no other kind of fiberglass cloths.

WOVEN ROVING

Woven roving is much like woven cloth, except that it is much heavier and woven differently. Most lightweight woven cloths look like

*Throughout this book, whenever the word *cloth* is used alone, woven cloth is meant. Matt cloth is always referred to as *matt*, woven roving as *roving*, and the combination of matt and roving as *Fabmat*.

a typical tablecloth, while somewhat heavier woven cloths look like a knit shirt. But roving looks much like basket weaving, with heavy bundles of nontwisted strands of fiberglass woven loosely at right angles so that there is relatively a lot of space between individual bundles of strands. The spaces between the heavy strands allow resin to flow through and more easily wet out the roving.

FABMAT

Fabmat is a combination of matt and woven roving, held together by a binder of dried unactivated resin. It is very heavy to handle, being some 3/32" thick in a commonly available weight. Fabmat is actually composed of two layers: matt on the bottom and roving on the top. It saves handling time when the layup calls for a layer each of matt and roving, since you are actually cutting and fitting both layers at once.

Fabmat is a trade name, therefore not all distributors will use this name. Fabmat is very difficult to wet out and involves a great many air-bubble problems. For these reasons it is not recommended for use by the amateur; however it has been included to round out the discussion.

A COMPARISON OF VARIOUS TYPES OF FABRIC

The following discussion is a comparison of several important characteristics of reinforcement material. As you will realize, each type of cloth has certain advantages and disadvantages. Often by using them together, you can combine the favorable features of each.

STRENGTH

A material's strength, as most people understand it, is the ability of that material to resist breaking when pulled or hit sharply. By this definition, cloth and roving are considered to be the strongest fiberglass fabrics, Fabmat is rated second, and matt falls behind as a distant third. For instance, cloth is about 40% stronger than matt.

Which is stronger: cloth or roving? In terms of high fiberglass content (that is, less resin), woven cloth is stronger (resin only bonds fiberglass together, and otherwise does not add strength). In a laboratory test, cloth would be stronger. However, in actual operating conditions, roving has shown greater impact resistance in collisions.

Matt is composed of short strands no longer than two inches in length. Both cloth and roving have strands that run continuously the length and width of the cloth. Perhaps you think that the shortness of the strands in matt has to do with its relative lack of strength? Tests have shown that this is not the case, that there is no falling off of strength until the strands are reduced to less than ¾" in length. Matt is weaker than other fabrics because it absorbs much more resin; therefore, volume for volume, it has less fiberglass than either cloth or roving when saturated with resin.

Cloth and roving, however, are strong primarily in two directions only, that is, in the two directions of the weave. There is relatively little strength on the diagonal. This problem can be alleviated when several layers are used by orienting the layers differently, so they complement each other. On the other hand, matt, because of the randomness of the strands, has uniform (although lower) strength in all directions.

Gel coat, for all practical purposes, has no strength. Its purpose is to give the boat an attractive appearance and to form a waterproof barrier on the outside.

RIGIDITY AND BRITTLENESS

If you experiment with a cured piece of resin or gel coat that may have dropped onto a piece of paper, you will find that you can easily break it in your hands. It is extremely brittle and has very little strength by itself. Matt soaks up much more resin than cloth does. Because matt absorbs so much resin, it is heavier, weaker, and more brittle than cloth.

We say that resin and matt are brittle. A material that is brittle, however, can usually be called rigid. If you think about it, you will realize that brittleness and rigidity are two ways of talking about stiffness. The main difference is this: when you like the stiffness, you call it rigidity; when you do not like the stiffness or have too much of it, you call it brittleness.

Previously, we said that matt, compared with cloth, is brittle. Looking at the same characteristic in another way, we could just as well say that matt, compared with cloth, is stiff or rigid.

Some boats, if they were made entirely of cloth, would be strong enough, but they would flex and twist excessively. The same boat, made of matt, might not be strong enough but it would not flex and twist so much. This suggests that matt and cloth used together might have just the right qualities of stiffness and strength.

THICKNESS

When trying to make strength and stiffness comparisons, it is important to keep in mind how thick the various reinforcing materials are.

Matt comes in several weights: ¾, 1, 1½, 2, and 3 oz. per square foot. Thickness varies according to the initial density of the matt and the degree to which it is compacted at the time of saturation with resin. However, 1½ oz. matt is generally about 1/20″ thick, and 2 oz. matt about 1/16″ thick. These thicknesses are true after the matt has been thoroughly saturated with resin; prior to the application of resin, the matt will be about 15% thinner.

Woven cloth is available in a confusing welter of widths, weights, and styles (different weaves). However the most common weights and widths are 4, 6, 7½, 10 oz. per square yard and 38", 44", 50", and 60". Boat cloth that is 10 oz. per square yard is just about right for the majority of applications, and a popular width is 50". (Notice that cloth and roving are so many ounces per square yard, whereas matt is per square foot.) After saturation with resin, 10 oz. cloth will be only 0.015" thick (about 1/64"). It would take about three thicknesses of 10 oz. cloth to equal one thickness of 1½ oz. matt. Going back to the section on stiffness, the three layers of 10 oz. cloth would not be as stiff as the one layer of 1½ oz. matt.

Woven roving is available in 18, 24, 26½, and 32 oz. per square yard weights, and in similar widths as cloth. One layer of 24 oz. roving, when saturated with resin, is approximately 0.04" thick (1/25"). That means one layer of 24 oz. roving equals about three layers of 10 oz. cloth, or one layer of 1½ oz. matt. This one layer of roving would be almost as strong as the three layers of cloth, and somewhere midway between the three layers of cloth and the one layer of matt in stiffness.

Fabmat is available in 25, 34, and 38 oz. per square yard weights. The 38 oz. Fabmat, when saturated with resin, is about 3/32" thick, or equal to two layers of 1½ oz. matt, six layers of 10 oz. cloth, or 2 1/3 layers of 24 oz. roving. Its characteristics would be a combination of those of matt and roving.

Gel coat is sprayed on between 15/1000" and 20/1000" thick.

WATERPROOFNESS

Gel coat, being pure resin, is highly impervious to water. Matt, having a high resin content, also makes a good barrier against water, and is often used as a gasket when connecting parts. The matt is put on first very carefully to avoid gaps. Then roving or Fabmat is applied in strips to give strength to the joints within the boat which are out of view.

Both cloth and roving alone tend to leak easily because of the small holes between the criss-crossed strands. These small holes can be filled with several applications of resin, but that will require more resin than is needed to saturate the fabric.

Should water get inside the boat and gather on the rough inside of the layup, it will in time penetrate and soften the fiberglass, causing it to lose some of its strength. This loss of strength, however, is usually not serious, and internal water tanks are often built within the keel areas of fiberglass boats by using the hull sides as two of the water tank walls.

RESIN CONTENT

A typical matt laminate is about 25% to 30% glass and 70% to 75% resin by weight. In other words, matt usually requires three times its own weight in resin before it is fully wet out.

A cloth laminate is 45% to 50% glass and 50% to 55% resin by weight. In other words, woven cloth requires about its own weight in resin.

A woven roving laminate is 40% to 45% glass and 55% to 60% resin. In other words, roving comes close to using its own weight in resin for full saturation.

EASE OF USE

As discussed more fully in Chapter 2, matt can be either easy or extremely difficult to use, according to the situation and your experience. The beginner often finds it difficult to use.

Before it is wetted out, matt is stiff, making it difficult to drape over the work. However, when resin is applied, the binder holding the strands together dissolves, and the individual fibers are free to slide around, making matt very pliable and easy to push into sharp curves and corners. However this pliability can cause trouble if, through inexperience, you push on the matt too much or in the wrong direction while saturating it with resin.

Woven cloth, when dry, drapes very well. It has enough diagonal play to enable you to spread it over curved forms, often without any cutting. However, you will notice as you are spreading it out while it is still dry that it is springy and will not stay put in sharp corners of the mold; that is, it springs away as soon as it is released. Unlike matt, which becomes pliable when wet, cloth when wet does not become appreciably more pliable. Consequently, it is difficult to make cloth stay in contact with sharp bends in the mold. Also, because cloth will not stretch or contract like matt (fibers of matt can slide over one another or be separated somewhat), air bubbles sometimes appear from nowhere in the middle of a piece of cloth and necessitate either tediously working them toward an edge, or slitting the cloth. Despite these problems, most people consider cloth easier for the beginner to handle than matt.

When dry, woven roving drapes fairly well, but will not at all conform to sharp bends. Like cloth, saturation with resin does not increase roving's pliability, and in a similar way, air bubble problems are common. However, unlike cloth, roving is quite difficult to saturate thoroughly.

Although there are relatively large gaps between the bundles of strands that constitute the coarse weave of roving, the resin still has difficulty penetrating the bundles themselves, especially where they cross each other. It is often difficult to tell which portions of the roving are not thoroughly wet out until the resin hardens, at which time the unsaturated sections appear as small white spots. Such spots seriously detract from the structural strength of the roving.

Fabmat, being a combination of roving and matt, is almost as impossible to drape as dry matt is, and is just as stubborn when wet with resin. Fabmat is extremely difficult to saturate completely, much more so than roving. To wet out Fabmat successfully requires a generous application of resin to both the Fabmat and the surface it is being applied to. Air bubble problems are compounded because air bubbles can occur in two places — between the Fabmat and the surface being covered, and between the matt and roving that make up the Fabmat. Because it is so difficult to handle, Fabmat is not recommended for amateur use.

ECONOMY

As you may guess by now, when considering the relative costs of various reinforcements, you need to consider several aspects:

1. The cost of the material
2. How much resin it absorbs
3. How many layers it takes to equal another type of reinforcement
4. How much labor is required to apply it
5. How foolproof it is.

The fifth point needs some explanation. To use an example, Fabmat is very thick. Although it is competitive in cost with other materials, and although one layer would be enough for the boat and could be put on in much less time than the several layers of some other kind of reinforcement, it might still not be desirable because in practice you would find that you could not saturate it well and work out the air bubbles. The result would be a defective boat. Because you know you could not handle it properly every time, you might prefer to use several layers of some other reinforcement, which you know you can handle with ease.

Table 1 gives statistics for one square foot of popular weights of three reinforcements. In order to fairly compare them, you must compare like thickness, therefore extra columns have been added to make this comparison possible.

COMBINATIONS OF REINFORCEMENT

As suggested previously, it is often advantageous to use several kinds of reinforcement together.

Because of the slight fuzziness of matt, which enables separate layers to partially interlock, one layer of matt holds to another layer of matt very firmly after the resin in both layers has set up. However, one layer of cloth on another layer of cloth does not hold as well, and may delaminate in time after use. This also applies to roving.

In general the weakest part of a fiberglass hull is between the layers, with the layers separating from the impact of a collision first; and then, because the layers are no longer working together, they can be pierced easily.

Matt, because it acts as a good "glue," is often used between layers of cloth or roving to counteract this tendency to delaminate. Often a layup is planned so that a layer of thin matt and a layer of roving is put on simultaneously (hence the development of Fabmat).

The best way to put on a layer of matt followed by a layer of cloth or roving is as follows: Put on the matt first, wetting it out thoroughly. Then lay the cloth or roving on the matt while the resin is still uncured. The excess resin from the matt, which can be squeezed out of it with a

Table 1

	1 layer of 1½ oz. Matt	1 layer of 10 oz. Cloth	1 layer of 24 oz. Roving	1 layer of 38 oz. Fabmat	2 layers of 1½ oz. Matt	6 layers of 10 oz. Cloth	2.3 layers of 24 oz. Roving
Cost per pound ($)	0.60	1.28	0.55	0.68	0.60	1.28	0.55
Weight of fabric (oz.)	1.5	1.1	2.7	4.2	3.0	6.6	6.2
Cost of fabric ($)	0.06	0.09	0.09	0.18	0.12	0.53	0.21
Weight of resin required (oz.)	4.5	1.1	2.7	7.2	9.0	6.6	6.2
Volume of resin required (fl. oz.)	4.0	0.95	2.3	6.3	8.0	5.7	5.3
Cost of resin required ($)	0.06	0.02	0.04	0.12	0.12	0.11	0.10
Total weight of cloth & resin (oz.)	6.0	2.2	5.4	11.4	12.0	13.2	12.4
Total cost of cloth & resin ($)	0.12	0.11	0.14	0.30	0.24	0.64	0.32
Thickness of cloth & resin (in.)	1/20	1/64	1/25	3/32	3/32	3/32	3/32
Total cost of cloth & resin if allowance made for normal waste, solvents, etc. ($)	0.23	0.20	0.24	0.40	0.46	1.20	0.55

roller or squeegee, will be enough to completely wet out a layer of cloth, and will often be almost enough to wet out a layer of roving. The important advantage of this order of application is that by squeezing the excess resin out of the matt, you not only save resin, and therefore reduce both cost and weight, but also you will have a higher percentage of glass, avoiding the over-brittleness of matt. One note of caution: this method will work only if you follow the matt with the cloth or roving quickly so that the resin you used on the matt will be still fresh.

Some small fiberglass boats have the rough, inner surface of the hull molding exposed on the floor of the cockpit. Usually the rough surface is roving, which has been painted with splatter paint to camouflage the roughness. For a smoother surface, the inside could be finished with a layer of woven cloth instead of roving.

There are a number of instances in the construction of fiberglass boats when matt is used for special purposes. When making certain joints where there is no gel coat to give waterproofness, a layer of matt will help waterproof the joint, even though the strength of the joint must depend on strips of roving.

Some fiberglass boats have a few sharp corners. These sharp corners are difficult to reinforce properly with cloth, because the springiness of cloth prevents it from adhering to the curve properly. In such instances, it is advantageous to use matt to reinforce the corners, although cloth is used to reinforce the flat runs of the molding.

In almost all fiberglass boats, the layer of reinforcement directly against the gel coat is either matt or cloth. Then following this initial layer are one or more layers of roving or Fabmat. These are used because they are thick and save labor, as fewer layers of roving or Fabmat have to be put on than layers of cloth or matt to make up the desired thickness.

PRICES OF REINFORCEMENT

Although per-square-foot prices for several reinforcements were indicated in table 1, you will probably find it helpful to know what full rolls and other quantities cost. Also an example is given of how to do your own calculations to arrive at figures like those provided in Table 1.

PRICE OF MATT
Matt is seldom available in retail outlets. Defender Industries sells it in three weights and four widths. For an example, 1½ oz. matt 50" wide costs $1.70 per yard (linear yard), however the price is reduced to $1.42 if you buy 21 or more yards.

Industrial suppliers sell matt by the pound, and you must buy at least one roll. The price varies according to the weight; the lighter the weight, the higher the cost per pound, because of the extra processing time required to make the thinner matt. Typical prices are:

¾ oz. matt — $0.59 to $0.79 per pound
1 oz. matt — $0.55 to $0.59 per pound
1½ oz. matt — $0.50 to $0.55 per pound
2, 3 oz. matt — $0.50   per pound

The above prices are for one-roll quantities. Usually you can request heavy or light rolls, however usually there will be 200 linear feet on a roll of 1½ oz. matt, 150 feet on a roll of 2 oz., etc. Rolls usually average out to be from 150 to 200 pounds in weight, which makes them cost about $100.00 to $150.00 each. The per yard price of 1½ oz. matt 50″ wide from industrial suppliers would be about $0.65.

Example of Calculations for ¾ oz. Matt

A very popular weight of matt is ¾ oz., as it can be made to adhere to sharp corners where nothing else will work as well. When studying the following sequence of calculations, realize that such generalities as the one about matt needing three times its weight in resin for complete saturation may not hold true for your shop. Before getting involved in a large project, you should experiment to see if you arrive at the same basic percentages.

One square yard of ¾ oz. matt contains nine square feet of matt. Since you need about three times the weight of the matt in resin, multiply nine times ¾ oz. to get 20.25 oz. of resin needed. 20.25 oz. is approximately 1¼ pounds. Since resin weighs on the average about 9.3 pounds per gallon, divide 1¼ into 9.3 to get .075 gallon. Since there are eight pints in a gallon, multiply .075 by 8 to get .6 pint, or a little over ½ pint of resin needed. So much for the volume of resin needed.

To get the cost of the resin needed, multiply the 1¼ pounds of resin needed by the price you pay per pound. If you buy the resin by the barrel, and pay $0.25 per pound, you will spend about $0.31 for the resin needed to saturate one square yard of ¾ oz. matt.

PRICES OF WOVEN CLOTH

A 10 oz. boat cloth is just about right for the majority of applications, and a popular width is 50″. Retail outlets will charge you $2.50 and up per linear yard.

Defender Industries sells boat cloth in several weights and widths. Their price for 10 oz. cloth 50″ wide is $1.46 per single linear yard, $1.29 if you buy over 50 yards, and $1.18 if you buy over 125 yards.

A 10 oz. boat cloth, 50" wide, must be bought by the roll from industrial suppliers. Rolls vary in length but average about 120 yards. The prices per linear yard in one-roll quantities from industrial suppliers range from $1.00 to $1.12 per yard; that makes a roll cost around $130.00. Notice that this price is not substantially lower than the "over 125 yards" price of Defender Industries.

The above prices are for chromed cloth. As with the other kinds of fabrics, you must be careful to buy only chromed cloth for boatbuilding.

PRICE OF FIBERGLASS TAPE

Fiberglass tape is available in a 9 oz. weight, chromed, in the following widths: 1½", 2", 3", 4", 6", 8", and 12". The edge is especially woven so that it will not unravel.

A retail outlet will probably charge you $0.55 or more per linear yard of the 4" width. Defender Industries charges $0.28 per yard, or $11.30 if you buy an entire 50-yard roll in the 4" width. Industrial suppliers sell tape by the roll only; a typical price for one 50-yard roll 4" wide would be $9.25.

PRICE OF WOVEN ROVING

Roving is generally unavailable in retail outlets. Defender Industries sells it in 26.5 and 32 oz. per square yard weights. The weights most often used in boatbuilding are from 24 to 26 oz. per square yard. Their 26.5 oz. weight in a 44" width costs $1.89 per yard, or $1.62 per yard for over 40 yards.

Industrial suppliers quote the price of roving by the pound. In single-roll quantities, 24 oz. roving costs from $0.52 to $0.56 per pound. A thinner roving, 18 oz., used in some sailboats where weight is critical, costs slightly more: $0.56 to $0.60 per pound. A typical roll of roving weighs between 100 and 200 pounds, and has 50 to 100 yards, making the price per roll from $50.00 to $120.00 (usually you can request them to deliver either a small or large roll). Comparing this to Defender's prices, a roll of 24 oz. roving, 44" wide, priced at $0.55 per pound, works out to be $1.04 per yard.

PRICE OF FABMAT

Fabmat is not available in retail outlets. Defender Industries sells 25 oz. and 34 oz. weights. The 34 oz. weight in a 38" width costs $3.55 per running yard.

Industrial suppliers price Fabmat by the pound. A typical quotation is $0.68 per pound. A roll of 38 oz., 40" wide, Fabmat will weigh about 130 pounds, contain 50 linear yards, and cost about $90.00. The price per yard works out to be $1.79.

SUMMARY OF COMPARISONS

The following briefly summarizes many of the points discussed previously.

STRENGTH
>Highest — Cloth (roving runs a close second)
>Most uniform — Matt (but overall strength low)
>Most between layers — Matt (use as "glue" between others)
>Weakest — Gel coat

WATERPROOFNESS
>Best — Gel coat
>Next best — Matt
>Worst — Cloth and roving

RESIN CONTENT
>Least — Cloth (very strong but lacks stiffness)
>Relatively little — Roving
>High — Matt (makes it rigid and brittle)
>Highest — Gel coat (pure resin; very rigid; extremely brittle)

EASE OF USE
>Gel coat — Unpleasant, difficult to apply
>Matt — Easiest to use for some situations involving sharp curves, but can make a mess for a beginner
>Cloth — For flat areas is the easiest to use
>Roving — Difficult to wet out
>Fabmat — Difficult to wet out

ECONOMY
>Cloth — Most costly of raw materials
>Matt — Cheapest material, but uses a lot of resin
>Roving — Saves labor
>Fabmat — Saves even more labor

COMBINATIONS
>By using matt between layers of cloth or roving, you can reduce the excess resin in the matt, and can increase the interlayer adhesion, while retaining favorable strength, weight, and cost.

NONFIBERGLASS REINFORCEMENTS

The following sections discuss Dynel and Vectra polypropylene fabrics. The same polyester resin is used with them as with fiberglass fabrics, and the technique of using them is almost the same.

Neither Dynel nor Vectra polypropylene is used for the reinforcement of gel coat in the manufacture of reinforced plastic boats. This is because of their higher costs and lower strength values. They are superior for use in covering wood boats, however. The only supplier of Dynel and Vectra I am familiar with is Defender Industries.

DYNEL

Dynel is a synthetic fabric about one-half the weight of fiberglass cloth. It is compatible with both polyester and epoxy resins. It has good abrasion resistance, high tensile strength, is soft to the touch, and is not irritating to the skin when sanded. The most easily worked of the fabrics presently available, Dynel can be stretched around curves and sharp corners more easily than Vectra or fiberglass. However, despite its good tensile strength, several experts say it should not be used alone because of lack of strength. Except on small plywood boats, Dynel should be used only over a layer of fiberglass. It is recommended primarily as an overlay because it produces a slick finish when sanded, or a canvas-like finish when applied to walkways or decks with a minimum of resin. Also, it has high abrasion resistance, as it is four times as tough as fiberglass. Dynel is a very subdued tan or buff color before it is wetted out, whereas fiberglass is a silver color.

PRICE OF DYNEL

Dynel comes in one weight from Defender Industries that seems comparable to 10 oz. fiberglass cloth. It is available in widths of 38", 42", 48", and 60". Prices for the 48" width are as follows: $1.57 per yard when bought by the yard, and $1.12 per yard when over 125 yards are purchased. See the Defender Industries catalog for a further price breakdown and an interesting discussion of Dynel's properties and use.

VECTRA POLYPROPYLENE

Vectra polypropylene, another synthetic cloth, is claimed to be the lightest known textile fiber, and is one-third the weight of fiberglass, which means that it will add buoyancy to a boat (heavier fiberglass is about twice the weight of water). At the same time, this lightness makes layup difficult, as Vectra tends to float in resin, allowing air bubbles to form under the fabric. To avoid any air bubbles, you must use only a light amount of resin and keep tapping the fabric down until the resin cures. Another disadvantage is that Vectra holds its creases more than fiberglass, adding to air-bubble problems.

Vectra's advantages are extreme abrasion resistance and extreme lightness for its strength. It adheres very well to wood and is much better, therefore, than fiberglass for covering a wood boat. Like Dynel, and unlike fiberglass, Vectra is nonallergenic and does not cause skin irritation during sanding operations. Only polyester resin is recommended for Vectra. The color and appearance of Vectra is very similar to fiberglass cloth.

DESIGNATION AND PRICE OF VECTRA POLYPROPYLENE

Defender Industries sells Vectra polypropylene in two weights: a 4.3 oz. weight which is equivalent in strength to 10 oz. fiberglass, and a 10.5 oz. weight which is equivalent to 20 oz. fiberglass cloth. The 4.3 oz. Vectra will absorb about the same amount of resin as will 10 oz. fiberglass cloth.

The price per yard in single yard quantities of 4.3 oz. Vectra in a 50″ width is $1.62. If bought in quantities over 125 yards, the price drops to $1.09 per yard. The 10.5 oz. Vectra in a 50″ width sells for $2.60 per yard.

Both Dynel and Vectra are available in tape form. For a complete price breakdown and discussion of both, see the Defender catalog.

COMPARING THE SYNTHETIC CLOTHS

Tables 2 and 3, which follow, compare many properties of Vectra, Dynel, and fiberglass. As you can see, the prices of Dynel and Vectra are about the same, while fiberglass is less expensive — and it is a great deal cheaper in large quantities. Only fiberglass is discussed in the rest of the book. However, the techniques used with Dynel and Vectra are practically identical to those used with fiberglass, except for treating the floating problem mentioned previously about Vectra.

Table 2. Peel Strength (in lbs. per sq. in.) of Vectra
and Fiberglass on Various Surfaces.

	Plywood	Pine	Maple
Vectra	31.0	32.0	3.5
Fiberglass	10.0	8.0	1.5

The primary use of Dynel and Vectra is for covering wood boats with abrasion resistant layers, because they are tough and provide superior adhesion to wood. In the chapter on repairs, the peeling problem of fiberglass is discussed and a way is suggested to partially overcome it. However if you use Vectra, there will be no problem at all.

For the regular construction of all plastic boats, fiberglass is superior in strength, although if it absorbs water, its strength is reduced to that of Dynel and Vectra. However, under normal circumstances, this soaking would never occur as the gel coat protects the inner reinforcing layers from water penetration. But whenever you get a break in the gel coat, it is important to fix it immediately to keep water out of the inner layers. (However, you must allow the damaged part to dry out before effecting the repair.)

Table 3. A Comparison of Fiberglass, Vectra, and Dynel[*]

Property	Fiberglass	Dynel	Vectra
Number of times heavier than water	2.54	1.34	0.90
How wetness affects strength	Reduces strength almost by half	No change	No change
		(both of these as strong as fiberglass when wet)	
Tensile strength	79,000	61,000	89,000
Flexural strength	24,000	15,300	15,200
Toughness	.07	1.2	1.6
Abrasion resistance	Fair	Good	Excellent
Irritation when sanding & cutting	Some, varies with individual user	None	None
Peel strength (pine)	7.7	28.2	32.4
Typical small quantity price/yd., 38" width cloth	$1.39	$1.69	$1.59
Ease of wetting out	Fair	Excellent	Excellent

[*]Statistics are compiled from Defender Industries catalog.

As you can see from table 3 fiberglass is obviously inferior in toughness to Dynel and Vectra. Toughness refers to the ability of a material to withstand sudden shocks, such as caused when a boat is beached on a rocky shore. This is a different strain than that of a heavy load being applied gradually. Fiberglass can withstand heavier loads applied gradually; Vectra and Dynel can withstand heavier loads applied suddenly. In practical terms as far as boats are concerned, this means that Dynel and Vectra will resist scratching and marring better than fiberglass, but that they are not as strong (in the normal sense) as fiberglass. In normal fiberglass construction, the gel coat takes the brunt of scratching, while the fiberglass, which is inside the gel coat layer, gives the overall strength. Gel coat very graphically demonstrates the difference between toughness and strength: if the gel coat is unsupported at any spot (such as at an air bubble), it will chip out easily, but if supported it will resist scratching well.

GRINDING COMPOUNDS

A grinding compound is used on the mold after a part has been pulled and before the mold is waxed for the next one. It removes fine scratches and surface hazing, leaving a high-gloss foundation for the wax to follow. It is not a cutting compound. Although a mold should be waxed before each part is to be laid up, it is necessary to use a compound only every five parts or so.

RELEASE WAX

You must wax the mold before making a layup, both to maintain the high gloss and to keep the part from sticking. Be careful to use only waxes designed for releasing polyester-molded parts. An example of a good wax for this purpose is Ceara Mold Release Wax, a 100% carnauba-base wax, sold at $2.75 per can by Allied Resins Corp., Weymouth Industrial Park, East Weymouth, Mass. 02189.

MOLD RELEASE

You will probably not have much need for mold release, a thick greasy material that looks like petroleum jelly. Normally you will use paste wax in order to have a high gloss. However, where a gloss is of no concern, such as along flanges that will join or be hidden in the finished boat, or in such out-of-the-way assemblies as the daggerboard trunk in a sailboard, mold release is much easier to use than paste wax, as you merely smear it on.

RELEASE FILM

Polyvinyl alcohol (PVA) film is a plastic material used as a parting agent between the fiberglass layup and the mold. This material is water soluble and can be washed off with moderate ease. It is usually applied by spraying on a fine layer. If an even layer is sprayed on, it will maintain the gloss of the mold and result in a perfect part. PVA is used in industry for the fabrication of many small fiberglass parts, such as covers for motors or switch boxes. However, it is used primarily on new molds for the first three or four parts pulled, in addition to paste wax, to assure that the parts will come out. Later, as the mold is fully cured and the bugs worked out of the release procedures, PVA is usually not needed.

STYROFOAM

Styrofoam is an extremely light, rigid, polystyrene foam consisting of millions of tiny air cells that do not connect with one another, which prevents waterlogging. It was developed for the U. S. Navy during World War II, and has since been used extensively both as flotation for boats and for floating docks instead of steel drums, which rust. Styrofoam will not rust, rot, or corrode; it is not affected by either fresh or salt water; it is resistant to marine growths and organisms; it requires no paint or other coating and is practically maintenance-free. When you first buy it, Styrofoam is white in color, but it turns yellow from exposure to the sun; this discoloration, although it looks bad, does not affect its other qualities. If pierced or dented, it will still float.

Besides the discoloration, which means you should not leave it out in view, Styrofoam does have some other disadvantages. The biggest one is that certain chemicals, such as polyester resin, acetone, styrene, gasoline, and oil, readily dissolve it. This means it must be protected from contact with these chemicals. This presents a problem for the builder who would cover Styrofoam with fiberglass, because you cannot glass over it without dissolving it. If you want to enclose it in fiberglass, you must somehow protect it from the resin by using cardboard until it cures. Also, Styrofoam is very soft and is easily chipped away if something hard hits it. For this reason you must enclose it behind a protective barrier of some kind, unless it is so far out of the way it will almost never be bumped. However, this softness makes it very easy to cut on a bandsaw. You can cut a 7" x 20" section as easily as a thin piece of balsa wood.

One cubic foot of Styrofoam weighs less than two pounds, which permits it to support approximately 55 pounds of weight in addition to its own weight. When replacing a 55-gallon metal drum in a dock, only 14 pounds of Styrofoam are needed to get the same buoyancy as the 50-pound drum gave, for instance.

All boats, and especially those with heavy equipment, benefit from the installation of Styrofoam. The foam gives protection in case the boat ever has a hole punched in it and fills with water. Foam should always be placed as high in the boat as possible. If you place the foam low in the boat — for example, under the floor where there is a lot of out-of-the-way space — should the boat ever fill with water, the effect of the foam will be to turn the boat upside down. If placed high, the foam will float the boat in an upright position. Therefore it is recommended that you put thin slabs of it under the deck, and under the ceiling of the cabin.

An informative booklet is published by Dow Chemical Company, Midland, Michigan 48640 on Styrofoam properties and uses. Also Dow can supply you with the name of a local distributor of their products in your area.

PRICE OF STYROFOAM

Styrofoam comes in "logs" measuring 7" x 20" x 9' 0". Typical prices per log, bought in quantities of one, are from $13.00 to $17.00.

LIQUID FOAM

For some jobs you will need a pour-in-place foam to fill odd-shaped or hard-to-reach areas. Also you will use it to adhere solid Styrofoam to fiberglass surfaces, as described in the final construction steps of the sailboard in Chapter 2. There are many different kinds of foam, but the kind you most likely will be using is a rigid polyurethane foam.

To mix the foam and start the chemical reaction, you mix two liquids together quickly. Then you have only a few seconds to get the foam where you want it before it has expanded its full amount. This kind of foam will adhere to almost any surface which is free of oil or grease. It is resistant to most solvents, including styrene, polyester resin, and acetone, which means that, unlike styrofoam, you can glass right over it.

You need to have adequate ventilation while using liquid foam. The fumes given off during the reaction are poisonous.

Incidentally all of these flotation foams are different from the type of foam which is used to make mattresses and seat cushions. Cushion-type foam is a semifirm urethane foam. Pour-type foams are harder and less even in consistency, and furthermore are more expensive than normal foam rubber.

PRICE OF LIQUID FOAM

Liquid foams are generally very expensive, costing as much as $5.00 per cubic foot of expanded foam. They are available either as liquids to be mixed, or in spray cans. There are companies in some cities that specialize in spraying foam and can bring their equipment to the job.

BALSA CORE FILLERS

As will be explained more fully in Chapter 4, sometimes it is advantageous to use a composite laminate of a lightweight core covered on both sides of fiberglass, rather than a solid fiberglass layup of equal strength. Usually it is advantageous to use this sandwich construction method only when the part must take heavy loads and would normally be very thick.

The idea behind sandwich constructions made by covering a lightweight filler on both sides with fiberglass layers is much like that of the steel I-beam. In the steel I-beam, most of the stresses are carried by the upper and lower flanges. The purpose of the vertical web connecting them is to hold the two flanges apart and at the same distance along the entire length. If the web should buckle and allow the two flanges to move closer to each other (which they are constantly trying to do when under stress), the entire beam will lose its strength and collapse. Balsa blocks, or other filler material in sandwich fiberglass construction, do the same thing: they hold the two outer layers of fiberglass apart and must be strong enough not to collapse.

Balsa Ecuador Lumber Corporation produces Contourkore, a blanket formed of end-grain balsa blocks attached to an open-weave fiberglass scrim (see figures 4-6 and 4-7 of Chapter 4, for a drawing of Contourkore, and a typical application of it). Contourkore easily drapes over curved surfaces because the end-grain balsa is cut into small 2″ x 2″ blocks. If the surface does not work out to an even multiple of 2″ in one of its dimensions, the balsa blocks can be cut to fit easily. Further description is given in Chapter 4 on how to work with this material.

Balsa is the world's lightest commercial wood. It weighs on the average less than nine pounds per cubic foot, or about one-third the weight of the lighter common woods. However, for its weight, compared to many foams which are used as filler materials for sandwich fiberglass construction, balsa offers greater strength. The type of balsa used in Contourkore weighs about six pounds per cubic foot, which means that it gives a sandwich structure over 55 pounds of buoyancy per cubic foot, requiring just that much less Styrofoam or other flotation.

Some users have been worried that disease or rot might attack the balsa after it has been sealed in fiberglass, thus weakening the structure. However, extensive testing has shown that, even in wood which is known to be diseased or rotting before lamination, the disease or rot does not spread any further once the wood has been enclosed by the fiberglass. This is due to the antiseptic qualities of polyester resin. In a comparison of various strength factors among polyvinyl chloride foam, polyurethane foam, and balsa wood, balsa is the strongest, though the foams are only about one-third the weight of balsa.

Balsa core construction (Contourkore) has the greatest strength-per-pound ratio of any lightweight filler material and minimizes or eliminates secondary stiffeners such as ribs or stringers, thereby saving on both fiberglass materials and labor. My figures indicate that the use of balsa core material as a filler is economical for large sailboats and power cruisers such as those discussed in Chapter 4, but not for small boats, because adequate stiffness can be obtained from the number of layers which would have to be used to cover the balsa.

The coefficient of expansion of balsa is low, meaning that it expands approximately at the same rate as fiberglass. Furthermore balsa has sufficient elasticity to adjust its rate of expansion to the surface plys. It has compressive strengths to 2,500 pounds a square inch (end grain), meaning that it gives excellent impact resistance. Also, if a boat using balsa core material is punctured, water absorption is limited to the damaged area, because balsa has a closed-cell construction.

PRICE OF BALSA

Contourkore in ⅜″ x 2′ x 4′ panels costs $0.407 per square foot. It comes packed in cartons of 33 panels (264 sq. ft. total). This price works out to $3.26 per panel or $107.50 per carton.

Prices of other thicknesses and various quantities are available from the supplier: Balsa Ecuador Lumber Corporation, 500 Fifth Ave., New York, N. Y. 10036.

FOAM CORE FILLER

There are several types of foam available for use as a core material in fiberglass construction. PVC foam (expanded polyvinyl chloride) and urethane foam come in various densities according to the requirements of the job. Many of these foams are heat formable: they can be bent to any shape desired with the application of heat from a heat lamp, and will retain the shape when they cool. Refer to Appendix A for a special section on the use of foam with other fiberglass methods.

Most foams are unicellular, meaning that water cannot run from one cell to another. They can be cut with a razor blade. When fiberglassed on both sides, these foams make a rigid construction, often 30% lighter than standard solid fiberglass laminates of the same rigidity.

Foam in general is quite expensive. Consult your supplier for the price of the foam he handles.

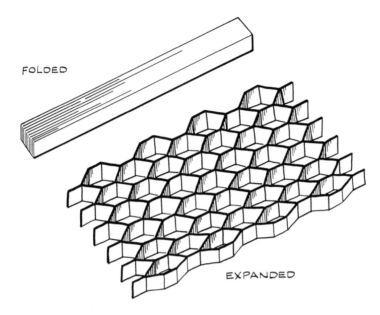

FOLDED

EXPANDED

FIGURE 1-1. *Honeycomb paper.*

HONEYCOMB PAPER

Honeycomb paper is cheap inner core sandwich construction filler. It is not as strong as balsa or foam and will crush more easily, allowing the tension surfaces to come together with a collapse of the strength of the section. However, it is good for noncritical applications, such as stiffening molds that are not intended for continuous usage. A serious handling disadvantage of honeycomb paper is that it will not conform to compound curves at all. Also, it is difficult to expand; it tends to return to its unexpanded shape and pull the fabrics laid on it into a glob.

PRICE OF HONEYCOMB PAPER

Defender Industries sells honeycomb paper in strips which, when expanded, measure ½" x 36" x 50". The price is $1.45 a strip, or six for $6.95.

THE SPRAY GUN

Spray-gun rigs, especially those designed especially for spraying gel coat, start at about $1,500 new. Such rigs deliver around 14 cfm (cubic feet of air per minute) at 80 psi (pounds per square inch pressure). They are designed to mix the gel coat or resin with activator in the proper amount at the nozzle, and have an acetone flush system for convenient cleaning.

You can spray gel coat with much less expensive spray guns, however. A unit that delivers as low as 7 or 8 cfm at 50 psi will spray unthinned gel coat, although with some difficulty (it will not be atomized properly). With even smaller units, you will have to thin the gel coat with acetone, using only enough to enable you to spray it (in no case should the mixture be more than one-third acetone by volume). Most of the acetone will completely flash off as the mixture is sprayed, so that only gel coat falls on the mold surface. Actually the acetone is somewhat detrimental to the gel coat, causing it to fail earlier in use (this is called *chalking*).

BARRIER CREAM

Barrier cream is a thick cream which, when spread on the hands, protects them from polyester resin. It continues to give protection as long as it is not washed off with water, and until it wears thin. An application gives up to two or three hours of protection.

Normally, you will want to wear rubber gloves for protection, as they are less expensive than barrier cream. However, for some operations, such as spraying gel coat when it is important to have full finger movement in cleaning out the spray gun quickly after spraying, you will want to use barrier cream.

Barrier cream is available from Defender Industries for $1.85 for a one-quarter pound tube, which will give several applications.

RUBBER GLOVES

Thin polyethylene gloves are available through Defender Industries at $1.00 for 16 gloves. They are as low as 100 pairs for $3.00 from some industrial suppliers. These gloves are extremely thin, tend to tear easily, and cannot be easily reused once taken off, as resin makes them stick together.

Heavy rubber gloves which have a thin lining are much better. These are sold in hardware stores for either dishwashing or general work for about $1.50 per pair. Even when cracks develop between the fingers after continued use, the lining will keep the resin out, thus extending the life of the glove.

BRUSHES

Brushes for applying resin should not have painted handles, as the paint will flake off from the action of the solvents in the resin.

LAMINATING ROLLERS

Laminating rollers are used to remove air bubbles from resin impregnated fabrics. There are two primary types: the aluminum roller, which has ridges; and the roller made of a combination of materials on which each little wheel revolves independently. The advantage of metal rollers is that, should resin harden on the rollers, you can burn the resin off. Radius rollers are used for sharp corners.

It is desirable to have a range of sizes of rollers, along with some radius rollers.

PRICES OF ROLLERS

Laminating rollers are quite expensive. A popular size, 1″ in diameter by 6″ long, sells for about $9.00. Some sizes cost as high as $20.00. Radius rollers average about $6.00 each. Radius rollers come in ⅛″, ¼″, ⅜″, and ½″ radius sizes.

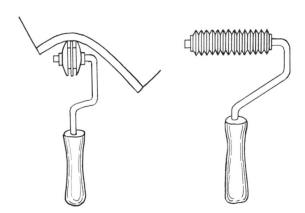

FIGURE 1-2. *Radius roller (left) and laminating roller (right). The wheels on both revolve independently.*

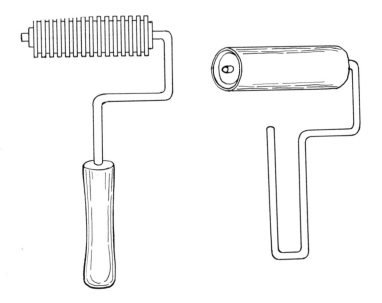

FIGURE 1-3. *Aluminum roller (left), and resin roller used for rapidly spreading resin (right).*

SQUEEGEES

Squeegees are used to scrape excess resin from layups (except when the top layer is matt), giving a higher glass-to-resin ratio for greater strength. Also they are used when applying resin to spread it quickly, and to work out air bubbles.

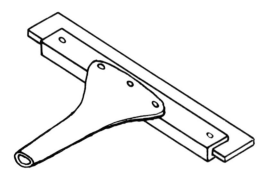

FIGURE 1-4. *Squeegee.*

TUBS

As an amateur, you probably will not have to buy tubs if you save all large food cans. However, large companies use disposable tubs or pails to hold resin. They are expected to last only a few batches before being discarded. These tubs must be unwaxed, because the solvents in the resins will attack the wax, which will contaminate the resin. For limited home use, clean "tin" cans will do fine. However, you must be very careful to remove all burrs from the rim of the can which may be left from removing the lid.

PATTERNS

One type of pattern is discussed briefly near the end of Chapter 2: it is a plywood pattern which is temporarily attached to a roughly sawn piece of wood. This pattern is used to guide a router, which trims the wood into a finished piece. In the example in Chapter 2, such patterns are used to shape the daggerboard and rudder. This is essentially a woodworking technique, and has only been included to show some of the steps required to finish off a fiberglass boat.

The other type of pattern used in fiberglass boatbuilding is to help precut in the correct shape the various pieces of cloth required for a layup. When many identical boats are being built, it obviously saves labor to be able to cut the cloth from a pattern rather than cut and fit it to the mold each time. Such a pattern is made by recording the shape of the cloth which resulted from the first cut-and-fit session with the first boat built in the mold. The shape is recorded on a piece of plywood, cardboard, or cloth; or it is drawn on the surface of a large table. Larger shops have a table which is reserved just for cutting cloth into proper lengths and shapes; it is called the cloth table, and rolls of various kinds of cloth are stored on a rack at one end of it.

SOME CALCULATIONS

Table 4 compares several different characteristics of various components of fiberglass layups on a per-square-foot basis. The use of this table is illustrated in the two examples and the comment which follows.

A word of caution: double-check all prices in this table before using any information in it to make a decision about a building project. As mentioned at the beginning of this chapter, prices that you can obtain may be different from those used in the computations which resulted in this table. Also, *and this is important,* studies have shown that different

Table 4. Table of Weights, Costs, and Thicknesses.

Type of material	Cost per pound	Fabric weight		Fabric cost	Weight of resin required		Volume of resin required		Cost of resin required
gel coat	$0.78	2	oz.	$0.10	—		—		—
¾ matt	$0.60	.75	oz.	$0.03	2.25	oz.	2	fl. oz.	$0.031
1½ matt	$0.60	1.5	oz.	$0.06	4.5	oz.	4	fl. oz.	$0.062
10 oz. cloth	$1.28	1.1	oz.	$0.088	1.1	oz.	.95	fl. oz.	$0.018
9 oz. tape	$2.56	1	oz.	$0.16	1	oz.	.86	fl. oz.	$0.016
24 oz. roving	$0.55	2.7	oz.	$0.093	2.7	oz.	2.33	fl. oz.	$0.044
38 oz. Fabmat	$0.68	4.2	oz.	$0.179	7.2	oz.	6.33	fl. oz.	$0.117
¼" balsa	$2.61	2	oz.	$0.325	—		—		—
⅜" balsa	$2.17	3	oz.	$0.407	—		—		—

fabricators use varying amounts of resin in their layups. Therefore, the amount of resin absorbed by each type of fabric listed in this table may be different from the amount you would use. To be sure of your calculations, buy small amounts of the various materials and try laying up several small pieces, carefully recording the amounts of resin you use.

Once you know the total number of square feet of surface area of a hull you are planning to produce, you can use the preceding table to compare weight, cost, and (in a crude way) stiffness of alternative methods of construction.

EXAMPLE 1.

The area of "Bluebird," an 18′ 1″ sailboat designed by William Atkin, is 175 sq. ft. Let's see what the cost, weight, and thickness are of the following proposed construction:

Layer	Thickness	Cost in $	Weight in oz.	Cost incl. allowances for waste, solvents, etc.
gel coat	.020"	.100	2.0	.18
¾ oz. matt	.025"	.061	3.0	.12
10 oz. cloth	.015"	.106	2.2	.20
¾ oz. matt	.025"	.061	3.0	.12
⅜" balsa	.375"	.407	3.0	.65
10 oz. cloth	.015"	.106	2.2	.20
Totals:	.475" (almost ½")	$0.841/sq. ft.	15.4 oz./sq. ft.	$1.47

$0.841 × 175 sq. ft.
= $153.18

15.4 × 175 sq. ft.
÷ 16 oz./lb.
= 168.5 lbs.

$1.47 × 175 sq. ft.
= $257.25

Type of material	Total weight	Total cost	Total cost incl. waste, solvents, etc.	Thickness	
gel coat	2 oz.	$0.10	$0.18	.020″	(1/50″)
¾ matt	3 oz.	$0.061	$0.12	.025″	(1/40″)
1½ matt	6 oz.	$0.122	$0.23	.050″	(1/20″)
10 oz. cloth	2.2 oz.	$0.106	$0.20	.015″	(1/67″)
9 oz. tape	2 oz.	$0.176	$0.25	.013″	(1/77″)
24 oz. roving	5.4 oz.	$0.137	$0.24	.040″	(1/25″)
38 oz. Fabmat	11.4 oz.	$0.296	$0.50	.090″	(1/11″)
¼″ balsa	2 oz.	$0.325	$0.50	.250″	(1/4″)
⅜″ balsa	3 oz.	$0.407	$0.65	.375″	(3/8″)

This construction will cost at least $153.18 and might cost as much as $257.25, according to how economically your shop operates. Probably a safe bet would be to plan on spending at least $200.00 per hull for materials.

An interesting statistic is that the factory cost of a typical fiberglass part, including labor and overhead, falls between $1.00 and $1.50 per pound. The hull, using the above construction, will weigh 168.5 pounds, which indicates that the price might fall between $168.50 and $252.75.

EXAMPLE 2. The same boat is to be built, but let's try this construction instead:

Layer	Thickness	Cost in $	Weight in oz.	Cost incl. allowances for waste, solvents, etc.
gel coat	.020″	.100	2.0	.18
1½ oz. matt	.050″	.122	6.0	.23
1½ oz. matt	.050″	.122	6.0	.23
1½ oz. matt	.050″	.122	6.0	.23
1½ oz. matt	.050″	.122	6.0	.23
10 oz. cloth	.015″	.106	2.2	.20
Totals:	.235″ (almost ¼″)	$0.694/sq. ft.	28.2 oz./sq. ft.	$1.30

$0.694 × 175 = $121.45

28.2 × 175 ÷ 16 = 309 lbs.

$1.30 × 175 = $227.50

This construction will cost at least $121.45 and might cost as much as $227.50, according to how economically your shop operates. As you can see, this construction is about $30.00 cheaper than the other construction discussed in Example 1.

The weight of this boat is high in comparison to the construction using the balsa core: 309 pounds. Using the rule of thumb about the finished cost including labor and overhead, we get an estimate of $309.00 to $463.50.

THE RESULTS

The construction used in Example 1 is almost twice as thick as that used in Example 2. Since stiffness increases as the cube of the thickness, Example 1 should be some eight times as stiff as Example 2, should weigh almost 50% less, and should cost about the same for materials. There is one undisputed advantage about the construction used in Example 2, however: you would not have to buy the expensive balsa core material, which could be the deciding factor if you were building just one boat.

You might try going through similar calculations for a construction using gel coat, 10 oz. cloth, ¾ oz. matt, 24 oz. roving, ¾ oz. matt, and 24 oz. roving. You will find that this construction compares favorably with the others.

You are probably wondering how the hull composition for each example was chosen in the first place. How thick should a hull be?

There are engineering calculations you can go through to help you arrive at the proper weights of reinforcement. These are discussed in detail in *Marine Design Manual* by Gibbs & Cox, Inc. However, the average small boatshop operator would use a "by guess and by gosh" method. First, he would take a walk to the nearest boat dock and see how thick his competitor's boat is. Then he would try to find how it is made by one means or another, that is, the weights, types, and sequence of layers in the layup (skill in industrial espionage is handy at this point). Then he would compare this data with his own experience with other fiberglass boats he has built or repaired. He might try building one, use it, and make modification after modification until it is right.

Of course, if he had a really sticky problem, he could always hire a competent yacht designer.

CONCLUSION

The preceding pages have described the various tools and materials used in fiberglass work, and have given you an idea of what you could expect to pay for them, comparing a marine supply house to various industrial distributors. In many cases, the prices of Defender Industries have seemed high, very high in comparison to industrial distributors, but you must remember that discounts available from an industrial distributor require large purchases, and in some instances such distributors will not even do business with you unless you are an established concern.

You may have some difficulty obtaining the names and addresses of industrial distributors in your area. You will not always find them listed in the Yellow Pages. You can learn their names if you can get a local boatbuilder or repair yard to give you the information. However, you may find this difficult because the boatbuilder may want to sell you your supplies out of his inventory, at prices considerably lower than the local marine supply store, but still higher than what he paid for them. And he reaps a double benefit, as the extra volume he purchases from the distributor entitles him to lower prices from the distributor.

You can learn the names of companies manufacturing resins and cloths from such trade magazines as *Boating Industry, Boat Construction/ Maintenance* and *Modern Plastics.*

Boating Industry is free to qualifying businesses, and otherwise costs $15.00 per year, ordered from Boating Industry, 205 East 42nd Street, New York, N. Y. 10017. *Boat Construction/Maintenance,* published monthly except July and December, is free to qualifying businesses, and costs $10.00 a year for others. It can be ordered from Boat Construction and Maintenance, 310 Madison Avenue, New York, N. Y. 10017. *Modern Plastics,* issued monthly, costs $10 a year. This price includes the annual "Encyclopedia Issue", which has about 1,300 pages and lists hundreds of manufacturers in all the various plastics fields, of which hand-layup fiberglass construction is just one little area. The magazine can be ordered from Modern Plastics, P.O. Box 809, New York, N. Y. 10036.

Below are the names of various manufacturers of resins who will be able to supply you with the names of local distributors on request:

Philadelphia Resins Company, Inc. 7636 Queen Street, Philadelphia, Pa. 19118. **Polyester resin.**

The Glidden Company, Third and Bern Street, Reading, Pennsylvania 19603. **Polyester resin and gel coats.**

Wallace & Tiernan Inc., Lucidol Division, 1740 Military Road, Buffalo, New York 14240. **Activator** (they call it **catalyst,** specifically methyl ethyl ketone peroxide).

ADM Chemicals (Archer Daniels Midland Company), 733 Marquette Ave., Minneapolis, Minn. 55440. **Polyester resin.**

American Cyanamid Company, Plastics and Resins Division, Wallingford, Connecticut 06492. **Gel coats and resins.** The following are their regional and district offices:

3333 Wilkinson Boulevard
Charlotte, N. C. 28208

3505 North Kimball Avenue
Chicago, Ill. 60618

10340 Evendale Drive
Cincinnati, Ohio 45241

111 West 50th Street
New York, N. Y. 10020

20545 Center Ridge Road
Cleveland, Ohio 44116

2150 Franklin Street
Oakland, Calif. 94612

7611 Carpenter Freeway
Dallas, Tex. 75207

185 Commerce Drive, Fort Washington
Philadelphia, Pa. 19034

15552 W. McNichols Rd.
Detroit, Mich. 48235

5025 Pattison Avenue
St. Louis, Mo. 63110

2300 S. Eastern Avenue
Los Angeles, Calif. 90022

4000 Aurora Avenue, North
Seattle, Wash. 98103

7630 Excelsior Boulevard
Minneapolis, Minn. 55426

South Cherry Street
Wallingford, Conn. 06493

Ferro Color, Division Headquarters: 4150 East 56th Street, Cleveland, Ohio 44105. **Gel coats.** Other service centers are located in:

5309 S. District Boulevard
Los Angeles, Calif. 90022

115 Skyline Drive
South Plainfield, N. J. 07080

1020 N. W. 163rd Drive
Miami, Fla. 33169

60 Greenway Drive
Pittsburgh, Pa. 15204

1439 South Harlem
Berwyn, Ill. 60402

601 Southwest Parkway
Arlington, Tex. 76010

Many of these distributors will refer you to firms right in your city or county which are local distributors for your area. When writing to these companies, it is well to write on a printed letterhead if possible, otherwise you may not be taken seriously. Expect to receive phone calls and other follow-up activity, as the distributors may at first believe you represent a large, undiscovered account. You will have to be able to buy large quantities and pay cash within 10 days for most to bother to do business with you. If they are reluctant to fill your order, which is usually small to them, you can offer to pick it up at the warehouse and truck it back yourself. Much of their objection to doing business with you as a home builder is that the quantity sold does not justify sending a truck to your home, especially since they cannot expect you to be a steady customer. You can remove this objection by offering to pick up your order yourself.

Unless you are really going into a large building project, you will not be able to utilize these industrial suppliers very extensively. Except for large volume items such as polyester resin, and perhaps cloth, it is best to order all the other items from a place like Defender Industries, which, while expensive in comparison to industrial suppliers, is cheap in comparison to the local marine supply store. A few items, such as thickener, are available in small quantities from IABBS Headquarters, 3183 Merrill, Royal Oak, Michigan 48072.

2/ MAKING A SMALL FIBERGLASS BOAT

Making a finished boat is explained in this chapter. It is assumed you have a mold. Making the mold is similar to making the boat, so what you learn here will help you understand how to make the mold when it is explained in the next chapter.

In this chapter, you will be shown how to build a fiberglass sailboard. This particular boat has been chosen because it is well known, and because it presents many of the problems involved in building a fiberglass boat.

In case you have begun reading this chapter before Chapter 1, you will have to refer back to Chapter 1 for the explanations of fiberglass materials and the basic ideas that underlie fiberglass construction.

Also, a word of caution about the organization of this chapter: it goes into great detail on each topic the first time it comes up, but only mentions briefly the same topic when repeated later. Several pages are devoted to each of the first few steps, followed by what is more or less a listing of the remaining steps that are repetitions of the first steps.

PREPARING THE MOLD

Before doing anything, you must be sure your mold is perfectly smooth and well waxed. (See Figures 2-1 through 2-3 for a complete mold.) The surface of the mold must be glossy just like the surface of a new automobile. It must be waxed and polished by hand to a high shine, using a good quality mold release wax. We will assume that your mold has no scratches from previous use. If it does, refer to Chapter 3, where repairing scratches is discussed.

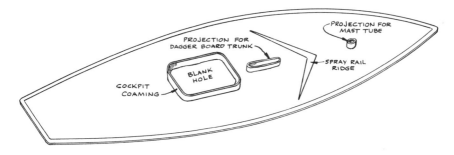

FIGURE 2-1. *Deck mold.*

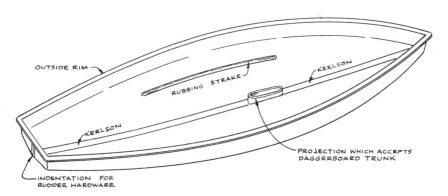

FIGURE 2-2. *Hull mold. The outside rim stiffens the edge of the hull formed in the mold and provides a surface for attaching the deck.*

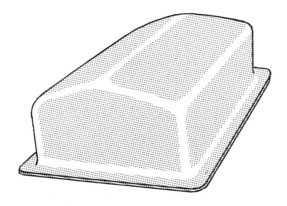

FIGURE 2-3. *Cockpit mold.*

Most mold release wax manufacturers specify that when a mold is first used, it should be given three coats of wax, each one buffed thoroughly. For the first three or four boats pulled from a mold, PVA should be sprayed on the mold over the wax to insure proper release. After the first few boats have been pulled, the mold is "broken in," and there usually is no need for PVA. Usually one coat of wax will suffice between boats thereafter.

It is imperative that you wax the mold thoroughly, missing no parts, and that the gloss be as brilliant as possible. If you do not do this, the boat may stick to the mold. It is much like when your wife makes certain types of cakes — she has to lightly butter the pan or the cake will stick. Besides sticking, any dull places on the mold will result in a correspondingly dull finish on the boat you pull out of the mold.

After you have waxed the mold, you must remove all dust from its surface. You can do a reasonably good job with clean lint-free cloth. It is not advisable to use an air hose because the stream of air could have particles of dirt in it which would scratch the mold. Furthermore the air under pressure could stir up even more dust. In your attempt to remove dust from the mold, it will help immeasurably if you have a very clean shop — otherwise dust may fall on the mold again immediately before you get a chance to spray. A big help in removing dust is a special tacky cloth manufactured by some suppliers. It has a slightly sticky, never-drying varnish which picks up all dust but does not smear the glossy surface of the mold.

THE GEL COAT LAYER

The first layer to go on the mold is the gel coat. This is the layer that you see when you look at the finished boat, and it gives the boat its color. Of course, you realize that you are building the boat inside out, starting with the outermost layer. What you add in the next steps will reinforce this outer layer which you see on the completed boat. The last layer added is the innermost layer which, in the sailboard, is hidden from view.

BRUSHING ON GEL COAT

If you do not have a spray gun, the gel coat can be painted on, but this is not nearly as satisfactory as spraying. If you must brush it on, follow these steps carefully or you may find your gel coat will "alligator," that is, form ripples or puckers.

Mix the gel coat in small quantities with at least double the amount of activator normally used for spraying. Gel coat is very thick and stiff, thus difficult to brush out thin, but it is imperative that you brush it thin.

Because gel coat is nonleveling, brush streaks will remain. They can be covered up by criss-crossing your brush strokes to some extent, but it will take four or five coats of gel to completely hide the brush marks.

Wait until the preceding coat has thoroughly hardened, not less than three or four hours, and then brush on another thin layer. The third, fourth, and fifth coats do not have to be brushed out quite as thin as the first two. This method of brushing is very laborious and therefore takes about 16 times as long as spraying. For example, a hull that takes one man 30 minutes to spray up completely will take two men working a total of four hours each over a period of three days to brush on an equivalent layer of gel coat.

SPRAYING ON GEL COAT

If you have a spray-gun rig, applying the gel coat will be much easier and quicker than by brush. Certain precautions, however, must be taken when using a spray gun.

Before beginning to spray, protect yourself with a cartridge-type mask and goggles, and put barrier cream on your hands. Completely cover up with a hat and long coat. Turn off all open flames. Avoid spraying outdoors, or allowing the spray to get outdoors, as the wind may carry it onto someone's car or house. Pour out a quantity of acetone in a pail for cleanup, and place it nearby so you can immediately clean the gun when finished spraying.

When spraying on gel coat, the object is to get an even layer on the mold about 15 to 20 mils thick (a mil is 1/1000 of an inch). That is not very thick, but thick enough to wear well and to hide anything behind it. If you put the gel coat on too thick, you will not be doing a better job: you will make it easier for it to chip off in the future, as it will be very brittle.

Proper Spraying Technique

There is a technique to using the spray gun (refer to Figure 2-4). You swing the gun not too fast and not too slowly from side to side, covering the entire mold systematically, overlapping each swing only slightly. At the beginning and end of each back-and-forth swing, the gun is off (not spraying). You do not pull the trigger until you have begun the swing, and you release it just before finishing the swing. The reason for this is to avoid building up a thick spot at the beginning and end of the swing.

If you keep the trigger on all the time, you will apply a double thickness of gel coat at the points where you reverse the direction of your swing. The reason for this is that you have to stop for a short time in order to move your arm in the other direction. Although you do not stop for long, it is long enough to spray the gel coat on too thickly.

Flat surfaces are easiest to spray, but be careful when spraying vertical or sloping surfaces. If you spray the gel coat on too thickly, you will get runs on these surfaces which will cause problems later on when putting on the cloth layers (the bumps of the runs make it difficult to get rid of air bubbles). But a more serious, and typical, mistake a beginner makes when spraying a vertical surface is not to spray it! You could miss a vertical surface altogether or put too little gel coat on it. This will cause ugly, dark spots on the finished boat — dark because the cloth that backs up the gel coat is translucent, and it is dark inside the boat. Figure 2-5 shows how this could happen.

Cleaning the Spray Gun

You must clean out the spray gun immediately after spraying, or you may ruin an expensive spray gun. Put acetone in the gun and spray that out for three minutes or more. Do not allow the acetone to hit the mold you have just sprayed. Then take the gun apart as much as you can and clean all parts. You should practice disassembling and reassembling the gun ahead of time before you spray. The reason why you must spray acetone through the gun immediately after finishing is that the gel coat is just like any other resin — it must be activated before being sprayed, and once activated, there is nothing you can do to stop it from setting up and clogging the small openings in your spray gun. Therefore, clean your gun immediately to get the gel coat out of the gun before it sets up.

If, particularly on a hot day, you should notice the gel coat beginning to thicken as you are spraying the boat (the spray will not come out as well as it should), stop immediately and clean your gun thoroughly. You can go back and finish the spray job, but your gun will be a loss if it is not cleaned immediately.

You should experiment ahead of time with the amount of activator to use so you know exactly how long you have to spray. It is important that you move along rapidly and finish the entire job in about 15 minutes to keep the gel coat from setting up in your gun. This is especially true in hot weather.

SPRAYING ON THE BLACK GEL COAT

If the gel coat you have just sprayed is a light color (and especially if white), you must go back and spray a thin layer of black gel coat over the light color. The black gel coat will not show through the lightest gel coat because all gel coats are extremely opaque. The black is needed to help you see air bubbles during the later steps in the construction, since air bubbles look white and will not show up against white or light gel coat. You do not need much black — just enough to make a gray color. Be sure to get a little extra black on sharply curved areas and around the rim of the molds, as that is where you could have air bubble problems.

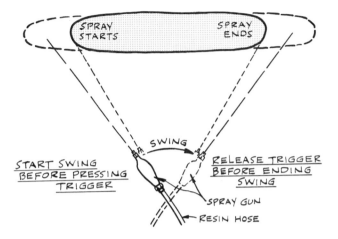

FIGURE 2-4. *Correct spraying technique.*

If the white (or light) gel coat is showing signs of setting up, you will have to clean your gun before spraying the black. On a cool day, you probably will be able to put black in the gun without cleaning out the other color first. Naturally it does not matter if you do not get a pure black because the other color is still in the gun — no one will ever see the black, and the only point is to get a darker color to cover up the white gel coat. After spraying the black, clean the gun thoroughly, which will remove the light gel coat as well as the black.

Although you spray the black gel coat directly on the light-colored gel coat before it cures, there will be no bleeding of the black through the light color.

MISCELLANEOUS COMMENTS ABOUT SPRAYING

A typical gel coat will require 2 oz. of activator per gallon for a 30 minute pot life at 70° F. At higher temperatures, reduce the amount; for example at 85° you would probably use 1½ oz.

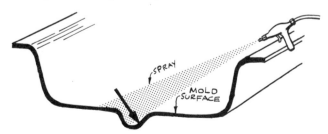

FIGURE 2-5. *Missing an unseen vertical surface.*

The use of a paint tank will enable you to clean your gun more quickly. Although tank manufacturers suggest that you pour paint directly in the tank, put the gel coat in a cardboard or metal pail, and put the pail in the tank. When you have finished spraying, pull the pail out, immediately put in a pail of acetone, and shoot the acetone through. Using disposable pails saves time otherwise spent cleaning the inside of the tank.

A common accident when spraying gel coat is to allow the spray hose to rub the mold. Some of the gel coat might be scraped off, leaving a dark streak in the finished boat if the problem goes unnoticed.

When you have finished spraying, avoid getting dust or dirt on the gel coat. In about 30 minutes to an hour, the surface will become tacky, and then you are ready for the next step. The gel coat is tacky when, although it feels sticky, no color adheres to your finger when you touch it.

PROBLEMS WITH THE GEL COAT

Occasionally, hideous blemishes appear soon after the gel coat has been applied. These are caused by what is variously called "alligatoring," wrinkling, rippling, puckering, or buckling. The blemishes appear more often after the gel coat has been applied by brush, but they also appear after it has been sprayed. The condition is the result of one or more of the following:

1. The gel coat was poorly formulated by the manufacturer.
2. The temperature during application was too low.
3. The gel coat was applied too thickly or unevenly.
4. Not enough activator was added to the gel coat.
5. The resin used in the reinforcing layer that touches the gel coat did not have enough activator.

The mold, air, and gel coat should be 70°F; however, it is better if they are warmer rather than colder than 70°F. Whatever temperature you are working at, the activator in the gel coat should be adjusted to make the mix as hot as possible. If it is too hot, however, it will set up too quickly and will be difficult to apply. The resin in the layer of reinforcement touching the gel coat should be mixed rather hot also so that it will be tacky in about 30 minutes after mixing. Be sure to stir the activator in both the gel coat and resin thoroughly so that all will be evenly mixed.

Depressions in the mold where gel coat might accumulate in a thick puddle are subject to alligatoring. Make every attempt to keep the gel coat at a constant thickness over all the mold.

Some people believe that waiting too long between spraying the gel coat and applying the reinforcing layers can cause alligatoring. In my experiments this does not seem to be a factor, however it is good practice to finish the boat quickly once work has begun, with the exception of large boats with very thick laminates where the heat given off by the curing resin would be too great. In practice, small boats often receive all the reinforcement at once, with successive layers being laid onto the wet layer just put down.

The layer of reinforcing which touches the gel coat can alligator if it remains uncured for several hours. In some instances, the condition can cause permanent damage to the mold as the uncured resin first buckles the gel coat, and then drips between the broken surface of the gel coat onto the mold surface. These little specks of resin adhere tenaciously to the mold despite thorough waxing and spraying with PVA. This is because they are too small to be grasped in order to break them off the mold. In an instance when this happened to me, the specks of resin could not be removed until I used a chisel and hammer to knock them off. To avoid this, always use enough activator in the first reinforcing layers, and mix it thoroughly, so that it has a cure time of about 30 minutes.

REINFORCING THE GEL COAT

Certain portions of almost every fiberglass boat need special reinforcement. There are two types of places that need this special reinforcement. The first are all the areas which receive extra-rough treatment when the boat is used. This would include such areas as the rims and edges which do not have much support and are often bumped. It also includes the rub strakes on the bottom of the hull.

The second type of place that needs special reinforcement is any area that will not be covered by the final layer of roving (the heavy strength layer). This also usually includes all small rims, as well as deep hollows, and the bottoms of steep bumps in the mold surface. Such areas do not get the roving layer, not because it could not be done, but because it is too difficult in practice to bend the roving around sharp corners and make it lie tightly against the areas in question. Since these areas are not going to be covered by roving, you add a special reinforcing patch of light matt to take the roving's place. This is shown in Figure 2-6.

You will notice as you build your boat that most of the places that need matt reinforcing patches need them for both of the reasons indicated above.

The important thing to remember is that the gel coat *must* be backed everywhere. If it is not, after the boat is pulled from the mold and put into use, the gel coat will break out if it is struck where it is not backed. This broken gel coat will leave a rough spot on your boat where you can see the reinforcing material. See Figures 2-7 through 2-12.

PLACES ON A SAILBOARD THAT NEED SPECIAL MATT REINFORCEMENT

After studying Figures 2-7 through 2-12, you should have a good idea of the parts of a boat which will need special matt reinforcing patches. However, since we are studying how to build a sailboard, we will list all the areas on this type of boat which need this special attention. Refer to Figures 2-1 and 2-2 for the location of the details.

Hull
Both aft corners — Figure 2-13.
Aft amidships, where rudder is attached — Figure 2-14.
Bow — Figure 2-15.
Beginning and ends of rubbing strakes, four patches — Figure 2-15.
Daggerboard trunk slot, two or more pieces must be worked together — Figures 2-16 through 2-18.
Along flange (rim), four or more pieces — Figure 2-19.

Deck
Mast tube opening, three or more pieces — Figure 2-20.
Cockpit opening, four or more pieces — Figures 2-21 and 2-22.
Spray rail edge, two or more pieces — Figures 2-23 through 2-25.

Cockpit
Along rim attached to deck, four or more pieces — Figure 2-1.
All four corners — Figure 2-1.

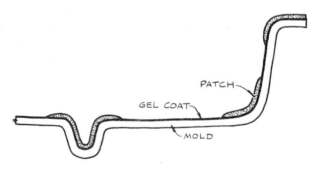

FIGURE 2-6. *Places needing special reinforcement, with patches applied correctly.*

If you count all these patches, you will see that you have in excess of 31 patches, all of which require your special attention. If necessary, you can cut some of the long patches on the various rims into smaller sections for easier application.

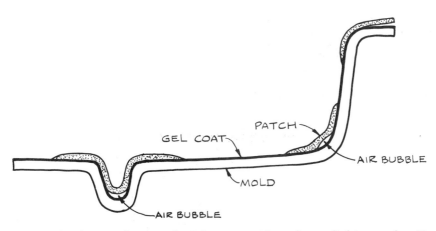

FIGURE 2-7. *Places needing special reinforcement with patches applied incorrectly. Air bubbles and loose areas under the patches will not support the gel coat.*

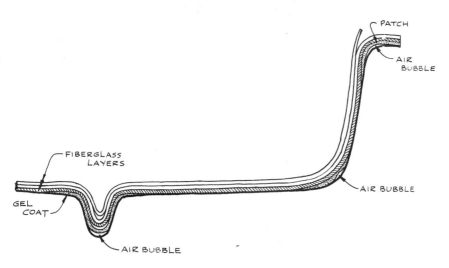

FIGURE 2-8. *Hull cross-section after it has been pulled from the mold.*

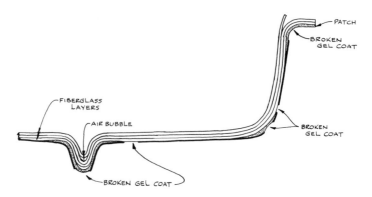

FIGURE 2-9. *Deterioration of the gel coat after the hull has been used. Unsupported areas have broken.*

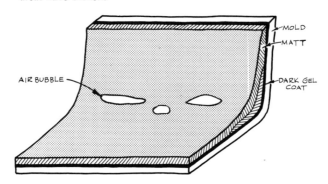

FIGURE 2-10. *Air bubbles in the first layer of fiberglass matt. Since the air bubbles form where the cloth does not touch the gel coat, they appear light in color.*

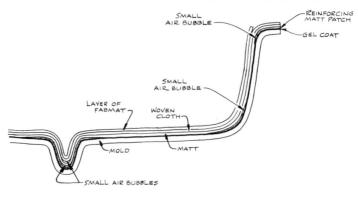

FIGURE 2-11. *Small air bubbles of minimum acceptability. They might cause trouble.*

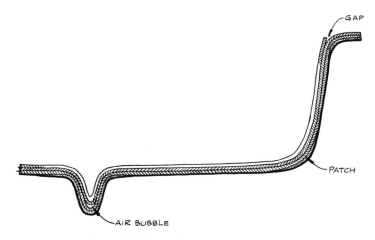

FIGURE 2-12. *Permissible air bubbles and gaps.*

FIGURE 2-13. *Aft corner of a hull mold with a matt patch in place. The gel coat is not shown.*

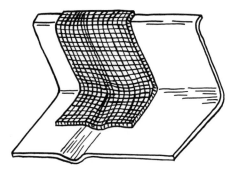

FIGURE 2-14. *Aft amidship of a hull mold with a matt patch in place. The gel coat is not shown.*

63

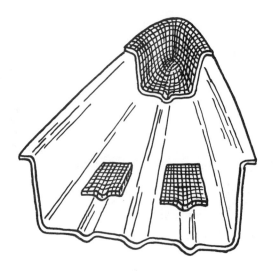

FIGURE 2-15. *Forward half of a hull mold with a bow patch and strake patches in place. The gel coat is not shown.*

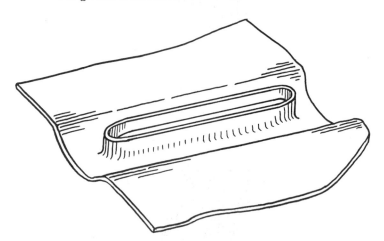

FIGURE 2-16. *Daggerboard trunk slot.*

FIGURE 2-17. *Cross-section of daggerboard trunk slot.*

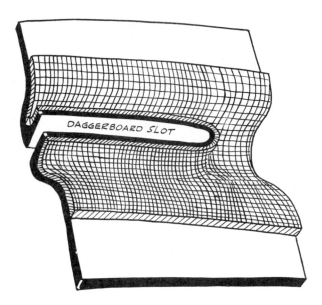

FIGURE 2-18. *Daggerboard slot area of a hull mold with the matt patch in place. The gel coat is not shown. The daggerboard trunk fits over the rim formed here by the hull mold.*

FIGURE 2-19. *Hull mold with roving in place. The roving is applied over the matt layer on first one half and then the other half of the mold and is overlapped about 2" along the centerline of the hull. For additional strength, lengthwise matt reinforcing patches have been applied under the matt layer along the chine and the rim.*

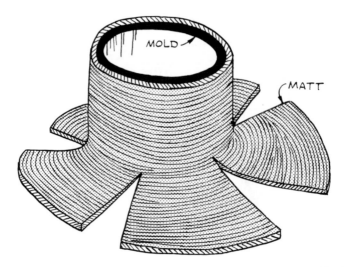

FIGURE 2-20. *Mast tube opening with matt in place. Although matt usually does not require slits to make it fit curved areas, a sharply curved area such as this does require a few slits. The edges of the slits should be tapered to avoid air bubbles in the layer that will cover this one.*

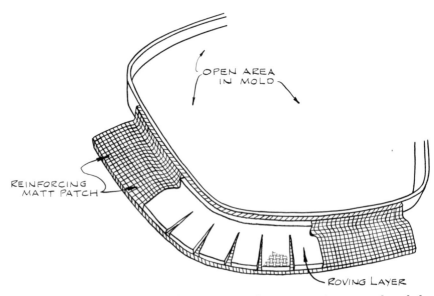

FIGURE 2-21. *Cutaway of the cockpit opening with a matt reinforcing patch and the roving layer in place. The roving must be slitted to fit the curve of the mold. The matt also may require slitting. The overall matt layer and gel coat are not shown.*

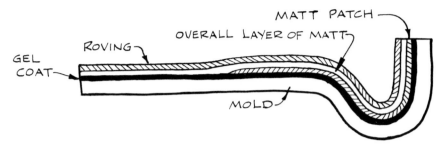

FIGURE 2-22. *Cross-section of the cockpit-opening rim showing all layers in place.*

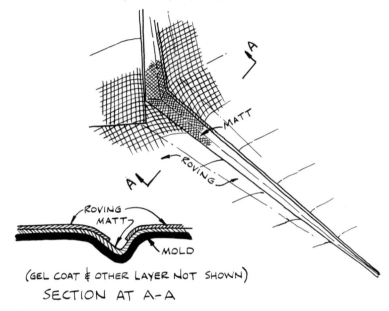

FIGURE 2-23. *Spray-rail ledge with overall matt layer and roving in place.*

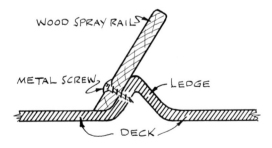

FIGURE 2-24. *Cross-section of ledge with wood spray rail attached.*

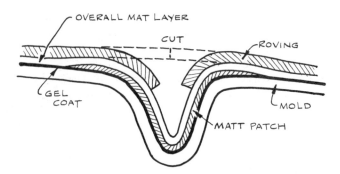

FIGURE 2-25. *Cross-section of the spray-rail ledge showing the application of roving. The roving is laid across the depression in the mold. It is cut, and then pushed down with a brush.*

APPLYING THE MATT REINFORCEMENT

So far you have learned where the patches must go and what they look like in place. Getting them in place correctly may be difficult for you the first few times.

You will find that there is some confusion in many books and articles on whether matt or woven cloth is easier to handle — most writers say woven cloth is easier to handle. Matt, when dry, is stiff and hard to bend around sharp corners, whereas woven cloth is very flexible. If you wet out a piece of matt and play around with it for awhile, it becomes a soggy mass of unmanageable fibers. This will not happen to a piece of woven cloth.

This makes it sound as if woven cloth, not matt, is easier to handle. But, as someone who has used both matt and woven cloth extensively, I think matt is easier to work with. Cloth is easier to handle when dry and will not pull apart when wet, but it retains almost all of the resilience when wet that it had when dry. This creates difficult problems wherever cloth must go over sharply curved areas. When the resin is setting up faster than you thought it would, the stubbornness of cloth, which just will not stay put when it is brushed, is a real nuisance.

Matt, however, is different. Because it is composed of short strands, it will bend when wet with resin to almost any shape you want it to assume. Unlike woven cloth, it will stay in place because the strands are able to slide past each other. All but the sharpest curves can be covered easily with matt, and no air bubbles will surreptitiously pop up when you are doing something else.

Using matt to best advantage requires experience. Those who speak of the difficulties of working with matt probably have the beginner in mind. You can easily make a mess of it, and will undoubtedly need to make a few boats before you finally get the hang of handling matt.

The secret of success is to use a minimum of brush strokes as you are wetting the matt out, and to think out each brush stroke so that it will be applied in the right direction and with the correct amount of pressure. Often small jabbing motions are useful, whereas in other situations they might make a mess of things. You will have to learn through experience, though, because it is practically impossible to teach brush technique by writing about it.

In any event, because matt is so pliable when wet, it should be used for reinforcing patches (¾ oz. weight is good).

If you touch the gel coat an hour or so after it has been sprayed, you will find that it remains tacky after setting up. In fact it will remain tacky for two or three days until it finally hardens.

At first this characteristic of the gel coat may seem a disadvantage (and if you did not know about it, you might think there was something wrong with it). But, if you use this gel coat tackiness correctly, you will find it a big help. You will notice that, as you place a piece of matt cloth on the tacky gel coat, it will stick to it somewhat. If you do not like where you positioned it, you can easily pull it away, although a very thick layer of strands will remain. When you try to get the matt to stick again after repositioning it, it will not stick at all, or at least not very well.

When you are ready to put in one of the many reinforcing patches needed, cut it roughly to size, and cut the various slits, which will enable you to fold the patch so that it will roughly conform to the contour of the area to be reinforced. To get an idea of how to cut the slits, look ahead to the drawings which show how to cut similar slits for the woven cloth which goes over these same areas.

Often the areas that need reinforcing are vertical, and here the little patches would fall down if it were not for the tacky quality of the gel coat. The tackiness is like an extra hand holding the patch in place, so you can use one hand to wield the brush and the other hand to smooth out the patch.

MIXING THE RESIN

Table 5 gives approximate gelation (cure) times for many standard polyester boat resins using a standard-strength MEK peroxide. However the indicated times, given in minutes, may not necessarily be accurate for the particular resin and catalyst you are using. Follow the manufacturer's instructions and make experiments in order to find the exact cure rate of the resin you are using. This is important — otherwise you may ruin a large job if the resin either cures too fast or too slowly.

The times in bold face are the ones you will probably find most convenient to use. For example, if it is 70°F in your shop, you would use

Table 5. Resin cure times.

Percent MEK peroxide by weight	Fluid ounces MEK peroxide per gal.	Temperatures				
		60°F	70°F	80°F	90°F	100°F
2.0	3.0	33	—	—	—	—
1.5	2.25	42	—	—	—	—
1.0	1.5	54	28	—	—	—
0.5	0.75	115	53	35	24	19
0.4	0.6	150	62	43	30	20
0.3	0.45	185	75	60	40	25
0.2	0.3	—	92	62	43	26

1½ fluid ounces of activator per gallon of resin to get a pot life of about 28 minutes. Actually, the amount of time you would have before the resin gets too thick to brush out effectively would probably be only around 18 minutes. This means you will have to mix small batches often.

You may think it would be advantageous to use less activator and mix larger batches, however this is less desirable for at least six reasons. First, having to stop every 15 minutes gives you a short break from the difficult work of laying up a boat. You can have a new batch mixed up and be back on the job before the last of the resin you just applied has fully set up, thus preserving your "wet edge," which is discussed later. Second, by mixing a small batch, the pail is not as heavy to hold. Third, when you have finished the task, you will not have to wait around very long for the resin to cure. You can be back working on the next step in about the time that it will take you to gather the necessary materials. Fourth, if you should have to stop unexpectedly in the middle of the job, you will lose less resin (which will cure in the can anyway). Fifth, if you should overestimate the amount of activator to mix with the resin, you will lose less resin if it should suddenly set up in your can as you are using it. And sixth, which is related to the fifth reason, resin actually sets up faster when in a large volume in a can waiting to be used, than if spread out on a surface.

House paint dries by evaporation and therefore will dry faster when spread out in a surface than when in a can; polyester resin, however, cures faster when it gets hot. While resin is in the can, the heat of the ongoing cure accumulates in the resin, making it set up more quickly than resin that is spread out on the boat and cooled by the air. Therefore, if you mix a large volume of resin with the proper amount of activator for it to set up in 40 minutes, it may begin getting sluggish in the can in 25 minutes; meanwhile, the same resin that you have managed to spread on the boat during that 25 minutes will still be fluid. If you use small batches of resin with relatively large amounts of activator, then, you can still mix up a new batch of resin and be back on the job in time to preserve the wet edge.

Because resin cures less quickly when spread out, some workers prefer to pour their activated resin in a large, shallow pan. Although such a pan is awkward to work from, the resin will last longer than in an easier-to-carry pail.

APPLYING RESIN

Once the piece of matt is stuck to the gel coat, roughly in place, slop on activated resin generously. There is no need to be neat here — the object is to get the matt cloth patch completely wet quickly. You will undoubtedly spill some excess resin around — you can brush that up later. It is important when doing this work not to waste time on unessential details as the resin will begin to set up quickly, and once the resin begins to get sluggish, you had better have the patch on correctly. Work quickly so you will be done before the resin begins to get hard.

AIR BUBBLES

When the matt cloth is wet, but not in complete contact with the gel coat, it will appear white or whitish. But when you push the wet matt hard against the gel coat, the color of the gel coat will show through the matt. If the gel coat is black, the matt will appear a very dark gray. Now perhaps you can see the reason for spraying black gel coat over the white gel coat: if you put the matt over white gel coat, you could not tell by a change in color when the matt was in contact with the gel coat.

This operation is very important. You must get the matt reinforcing patch, every bit of it, in contact with the gel coat underneath. Figure 2-9 shows what will happen if you allow the matt to stand away from the gel coat it is supposed to reinforce; you will have an air bubble, and the gel coat will crack and break away the first time it is hit sharply. This means you will lose both the smooth surface and the waterproof layer. The reinforcing layers are much more water absorbent than the gel coat.

Air bubbles cannot be seen once the boat is completed. Avoiding them is largely a matter of the worker's integrity. The layers next to the gel coat should have no air bubbles at all. The farther the layer from the gel coat, the more air bubbles can be tolerated. It would be too much labor to work out all the air bubbles throughout the boat.

Perhaps you can see that the fiberglass boat you buy can look beautiful, but be full of air bubbles that you will not discover until you hit one of them on something. Such weak areas may continue popping up for months because you will not hit all of them the first time you slide your boat up the beach. You, as an amateur boatbuilder, should be willing to spend the time and patience to work out all air bubbles in the layers which touch the gel coat.

WORKING OUT AIR BUBBLES WHILE APPLYING RESIN

Spraying the gel coat is the most unpleasant task in making most fiberglass boats because of all the protective gear you must wear, and the demanding aspect of having to get the gel coat on perfectly while working as fast as possible. But chasing down air bubbles often is the most frustrating and exasperating job.

After the matt is thoroughly wet, hold your brush at a low angle (see Figure 2-26) and, applying considerable pressure, pull the brush toward the edge of the matt. Repeat this several times, always starting near the middle and brushing to a different portion of the matt edge. This action will smooth the matt and compact it, and will force air that might be under the matt out to the sides.

Those bubbles which are left should be jabbed several times. Hit straight down on the bubble with the tip of the brush, hitting it hard (you need a stiff bristle brush for this to work). See Figure 2-27 for this jabbing motion.

When jabbing at an air bubble, always hit it from straight above. If you hit it at an angle, you will disturb the matt, pushing it to one side where it will lump up. Smooth the surface after every couple of jabs by brushing over it at a low angle with considerable force as described previously.

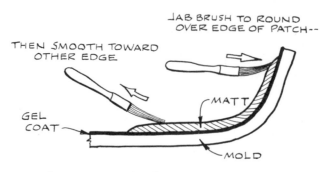

FIGURE 2-26. *Working a taper into the edge of a reinforcing patch.*

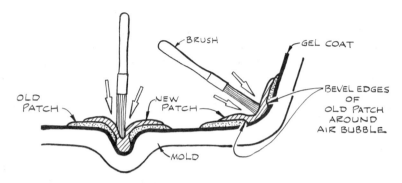

FIGURE 2-27. *Patching an air bubble.*

The effect of the jabs will be to break up the air bubble into several smaller ones. If the bubble is no larger than a pin head, you may leave it.

Another good method of getting rid of air bubbles after wetting out matt is to use a resin roller. Before the resin begins to set up, the roller can be rolled from the middle of the piece of matt to the edges, forcing the air out to one side. For the little reinforcing patches being described here, most rollers are much too big, however if you have a small radius roller you may be able to use it to some advantage. A roller is really of more use for big pieces of matt, and the methods of removing air bubbles with the brush suffice quite well for little patches.

The first time you try working out air bubbles, do not expect to be able to do the job very quickly. You are likely to have to work very slowly, mixing enough resin for one or two patches and concentrating on each step as you proceed. You must remove all air bubbles before the resin becomes tacky. If your resin gets tacky before you get rid of all the air bubbles, you will not be able to work them out. This calls for the annoying repair action described next.

REMOVING AIR BUBBLES AFTER RESIN HAS CURED

The best fiberglass worker will get an air bubble once in a while. Fortunately there is a remedy.

Figure 2-10 shows you a view of what an air bubble looks like after the resin has hardened. It is a light spot. To repair it you first must use a razor blade or sharp knife to cut around the edge of the air bubble, preferably before the resin has hardened completely, removing the matt cloth which is not adhered to the gel coat. You must be careful to remove all the cloth which is not adhered, and you need to be careful not to pull up any which is adhered (but able to be pulled up because the resin is still soft). If you can, cut in such a way that the edges are beveled.

After removing the air bubble, the gel coat will be exposed again, of course. Take a small piece of matt cut from a scrap a little bit bigger than the hole left by the air bubble. Position it over the hole; it should stick as the resin should be somewhat tacky (assuming you are making the repair before the resin has hardened). Use a small brush to wet out the patch thoroughly with resin and concentrate on making it contact the surface of the gel coat. Be careful not to allow new air bubbles to form at the edge of the hole where the patch is made. See Figure 2-27 for a visual description of how this is done.

As you apply these patches, and all the layers of cloth, you may want to use your other hand to help smooth the cloth, push it into place, etc. Most of the time however, you will not need to use your other hand as you gain experience. The exception to this is when working on vertical or overhead surfaces.

WATER MARKS

On occasion, you might see imperfections that look like air bubbles but, when you try cutting them away, you will find the cloth actually is in contact with the gel coat. That is, you will have a whole patch of white areas which are not air bubbles. This condition is a result of moisture in the cloth, caused by somehow getting it wet (perhaps there was water on the mold if you used water to clean dust off it), or by excess humidity. Normally you will find there was water involved rather than humidity. There really is no way to repair water marks short of ripping the entire area off, which I would say is not justified. These areas seem to hold fairly well, though not as well as those covered by dry cloth. You will have to use your judgment to decide whether to start over or not. This problem does not occur very often, fortunately.

TRIMMING

You will have to trim the excess cloth which hangs over the edge of the mold from many of the patches. Figure 2-28 shows the same patch illustrated in Figure 2-13. You will see that some of the matt cloth hangs over the edge of the mold and must be cut off with a razor blade or sharp knife, so that it is even with the edge of the mold. It is best to trim these patches just before they harden. If you trim too soon, you will have difficulty cutting, and you will move the patch, perhaps introducing air bubbles. If you try cutting after the resin has set up hard, you will need a hack saw to cut it, and you take a chance of cutting the mold if you cannot saw straight. When you finish trimming off the excess with a sharp knife, wait until the patch has set up all the way and then go over the edge with a sander with medium-fine sandpaper to trim the matt as close as possible to the edge of the mold. A careful job done here will make releasing the boat from the mold easier.

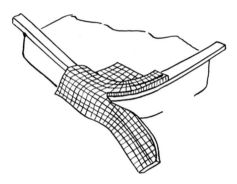

FIGURE 2-28. *Trimming a matt patch on the aft corner of a hull. Trim with a sharp knife when the cloth is fairly stiff, but not hard.*

An alternate to trimming as described above is to cut all layers of cloth off about one inch beyond the edge, and let it harden. This extra inch will give you something to pull on in order to remove the boat from the mold, and can later be cut off with a sabre saw (or other rig) after the hull is pulled from the mold. If you use this method, you must prevent any part of the patch that projects out from drooping down and touching the outside of the mold; otherwise the edge of the mold will be sealed so you cannot pull the hull free.

The first method of trimming before pulling the hull is standard practice, however the second method works well in some situations.

FINAL COMMENT ABOUT PATCHES

Figures 2-6 through 2-28 should give you a very good idea of how the various reinforcing patches appear when in place. You will notice that some of them will definitely need a few cuts with scissors, such as the patch which goes around the mast tube opening in the deck (Figure 2-20). Others may or may not need cuts according to your dexterity. The thing to remember is not to make any more cuts than you need to get a patch in place. When you do cut the cloth, try to work the edges into a taper (see Figure 2-26). The reason for this is to avoid situations that will make air bubbles likely in the next layer (if the next layer goes over a sharp ridge, it will be difficult to avoid an air bubble right at the bottom of that ridge).

There is little reason to elaborate on the various patches involved in a sailboard. The drawings give you a very good idea of what they look like when you are done. However, I do want to mention Figures 2-23 through 2-25, which show the spray rail ledge, with both the matt layer and one of the next layers in place. When the deck is pulled from its mold, this ledge will be a sharp ledge about one inch high, one-half inch at the base, several inches long, and in the overall shape of a V. When molding this shape, you have to really push the matt cloth hard down into the hollow as it is very easy to get air bubbles in such a deep hollow.

THE FIRST LAYER BACKING ALL THE GEL COAT

After the matt patches are all in place, only the corners and places that have sharp bends have backing. The rest of the mold is still covered with only bare gel coat. Now you must place the first layer of cloth over all the gel coat. This layer will also cover the patches you have just put on, meaning that there will be a double thickness where the reinforcing patches are.

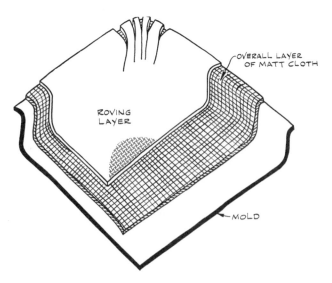

FIGURE 2-29. *Roving in place in the aft corner. The corner matt patch is covered by the overall matt layer and the roving layer. The gel coat is not shown.*

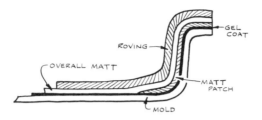

FIGURE 2-30. *Cross-section of aft section with all layers in place.*

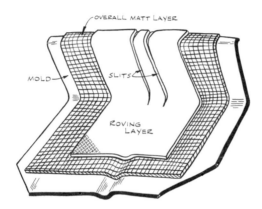

FIGURE 2-31. *Roving in place, aft amidships. The matt patch is covered by the over-all matt layer and the roving layer. The gel coat is not shown.*

Some manufacturers prefer to use a lightweight woven cloth for this overall layer because it is stronger than matt. But on any hull that has several difficult shapes to fit, such as the rub strakes, matt is a better choice because it can be easily worked into all contours, whereas woven cloth will be difficult to put on without numerous air bubbles.

For a sailboard, the rolls of matt should be ordered in a 48-inch width. Cut a piece a couple of feet longer than the boat. Starting with the hull, lay one edge of the cloth along the centerline. Rubbing the matt cloth with your hands, slowly push it against all the gel coat and over the reinforcing patches which are already in place. Because of the slight tackiness of the gel coat and resin, it will stick where you put it. Try to position it the first time exactly where you want it. The object of this layer is much the same as that of the reinforcing patches: to provide support for the fragile gel coat.

You will finally work this big piece of matt cloth over one entire half of the hull mold. You may well have to make some slits in the matt in order to get it to fit the contours, as shown in Figures 2-20, 2-29, and 2-31.

When you finish rubbing the matt down, it should stick to almost all of the surfaces, so there will be a minimum of air bubbles for you to work out with your brush as you apply the resin.

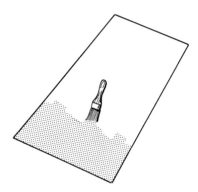

FIGURE 2-32. *The "wet edge." The dry matt is light in color; it turns dark when thoroughly wetted with resin.*

MAINTAINING A SHORT WET EDGE

With a surface as large as one-half of a sailboard, you cannot finish wetting out the entire piece of matt before the resin cures. Therefore, you must mix small batches. Start at one end of the mold, work out air bubbles as you go along, and proceed to the other end, maintaining a continuous wet edge. Put out enough unactivated resin in small pails on a bench, so you can mix more resin with activator as you need it. Refer to Figures 2-32 and 2-33.

The resin roller will help you to eliminate air bubbles quickly. Your resin should be mixed to give about a 30-minute pot life. You should work quickly, and the mold half should be done in 20 minutes. If you find any air bubbles after the resin has become tacky, you will have to cut them out and patch the holes.

This first layer which is next to the gel coat should have no air bubbles. Where this layer goes over the reinforcing patches applied earlier, you can be a little more tolerant of air bubbles, perhaps letting ones no bigger than a green pea remain. But on the places that touch the gel coat, you should repair all air bubbles unless they are no bigger than one-eighth of an inch in diameter and are an inch apart.

When you have covered one-half of the hull mold in its entirety with a layer of matt, and it has hardened, do the same for the other half, overlapping the matt along the centerline about three inches.

In a similar manner, you will probably be able to cover the deck with two pieces of matt cloth applied lengthwise, and the cockpit with two or three pieces. When you finish this stage, all parts of the gel coat will be covered with a layer of light matt cloth.

THE STRENGTH LAYER

The gel coat is the waterproof barrier, but it is quite fragile and must be reinforced at all points to keep it from chipping in service. The matt cloth, which is its direct reinforcement, is considerably stronger than the gel coat, and also is waterproof (however, it is more water absorbent than the gel coat). The layers which go on next are higher in glass content and lower in resin content, meaning they are stronger. It is the layer or layers that follow that provide the real strength.

For the sailboard, one layer of a heavy woven roving should be sufficient to complete the parts. This roving is about one-eighth of an inch thick, and is made up of strands one-eighth of an inch in diameter, woven loosely. Of course the large strands, themselves, are made of many, many fine glass strands.

This heavy woven roving is much too stiff to go into any deep hollows, or even adhere to all parts of other curved areas. Therefore such areas appear as large air bubbles when the roving is put on. There is no reason to try to work these air bubbles out, as the reinforcing patches provide the strength for these areas.

Since this particular boat calls for just one overall layer of matt and one layer of roving, it is probably best to allow the matt to cure before putting on the roving. Because of the fairly complex shape of a sailboard, putting the roving on the boat while the matt is still wet could result in your accidentally pulling the matt away from the gel coat and creating air bubbles. However, on many boats, it will be possible to lay the roving immediately on the wet matt, and the excess resin in the matt will help wet out the roving. It is even possible sometimes to roll both the matt and roving together to work out air bubbles, though this technique will require several people — you will need manpower to handle the bubbles and position the fabric before the resin cures.

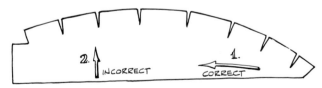

FIGURE 2-33. *Keeping the shortest wet edge. Always apply resin in a fore-and-aft direction, a section at a time.*

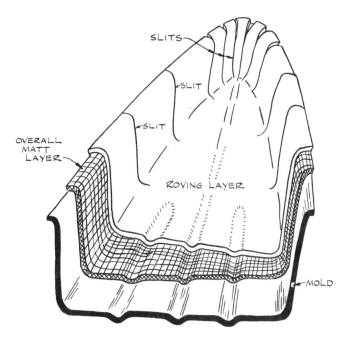

Figure 2-34. *Roving in place, forward half of hull. The gel coat and reinforcing patches are not shown.*

The heavy roving is laid down almost exactly as described for the previous overall layer of matt. The roving will definitely have to be cut to enable you to fit it over curved areas. Try to use as few cuts as possible, and make certain that the cut areas overlap, so that roving touches roving. If there is a gap where you made a cut, use a small patch to cover the gap after the roving is in place.

You will find the heavy roving difficult to wet out. Usually woven cloths have a silver-colored treatment which indicates when the cloth is thoroughly soaked with resin. When the cloth is thoroughly soaked through, the silver color will completely disappear. You have to slop the resin on heartily. It helps to get resin on the underside as well by pulling the roving back and brushing the layer which is already in place. Whereas one gallon of resin might completely wet out the lightweight matt which you covered one-half the hull with, it may take two and one-half gallons to wet the heavy roving out completely.

The same resin roller used to work air bubbles out of the matt layers is helpful in working out air bubbles in the roving layer. As with the matt, roll the air bubbles toward an edge. You will find it is much better on occasion to roll the roller quickly over the bubbles from several different directions, one after another. Flush the roller with acetone periodically to prevent clogging (roll it in a large, flat pan filled with acetone).

Apply the other pieces of roving in the same way so that the entire mold surface of the hull, deck, and cockpit, except for rims and hollows, is covered. Just as you had to trim the other two layers, any rough pieces of roving sticking up over the edge of the mold should be cut off.

When this roving layer is completed, you have finished the basic construction of the boat. On some boats you may need to apply two layers of roving. If this is done, you will get a better bond if you put a layer of matt between the layers of roving. To facilitate this technique, Fabmat, a combination of heavy roving and heavy matt, was developed.

In Fabmat, the heavy matt is held to the roving by dried unactivated resin. The two cloths are pulled off the roll together and cut and worked together, saving much labor. With this type of heavy combination cloth, you almost have to flow resin under as well as on top of the fabric during wetting out.

Figures 2-34 and 2-35 illustrate the roving layer.

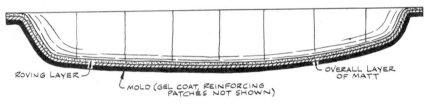

FIGURE 2-35. *Longitudinal cross-section of the hull with roving in place. The gel coat reinforcing patches are not shown.*

FINISHING THE BOAT

After the basic hull has been laid up, there are many additional jobs that must be done before the boat can be assembled. Each of these is treated in the following sections.

THE DAGGERBOARD TRUNK

One of the side jobs not mentioned earlier which must be done before the hull and deck are joined is the fabrication of the daggerboard trunk, illustrated in Figures 2-36 through 2-38. Figure 2-36 shows the daggerboard trunk mold, with the taper exaggerated. Although the taper on the actual mold is not easily discernible by eye, it must be there to enable you to pull the completed trunk off the mold. (A 2° taper is good; 4° to 6° is better.)

Since the trunk will be out of view, the mold need only be smooth,

FIGURE 2-36. *Daggerboard trunk mold. The taper is greatly exaggerated.*

not glossy. The daggerboard trunk is molded from several small pieces of matt which are wound around the mold and wetted out. The trunk should be about three matt layers thick, or about 1/8 to 3/16 of an inch thick.

After the trunk is removed from its mold, it is trimmed exactly so that it will fit between the hull and the deck when the boat is assembled. Figure 2-38 shows the trunk being attached to the hull directly over the slot formed earlier when the hull was molded (see Figure 2-16). You can see that the joint between the daggerboard trunk and the daggerboard slot is completely covered with pieces of matt, which waterproof this potential source of leaks. Then roving is placed over the matt to give strength to the joint. It is important that this joint be made carefully, as the daggerboard trunk must be able to take great strains when the boat is being used. Before you begin glassing the trunk in place you will have to be very careful to position it correctly so that it will join the daggerboard slot in the deck. When the trunk is in place, it will appear as in Figure 2-37.

Not shown in the illustrations is a flange in the upper lip of the daggerboard trunk. If you make a flange in the upper edge, you will be able to get a better joint between the daggerboard trunk and the deck when the hull and deck are assembled.

THE COCKPIT

When the hull and deck are joined, a drain plug hole will be cut through the hull and the self-bailing drain installed. The drain is designed so that it will drain the cockpit well when the boat is traveling forward at a good speed, but it will close when the boat stops. The cockpit well is attached to the deck as shown in Figure 2-39. Use matt all around the edge of the well to waterproof the joint, then add pieces of roving to give strength to the joint. At this time, you can also add some

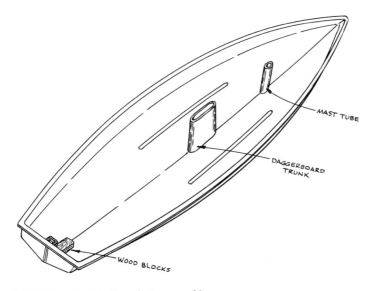

MAST TUBE

DAGGERBOARD
TRUNK

WOOD BLOCKS

FIGURE 2-37. *Completed hull ready for assembly.*

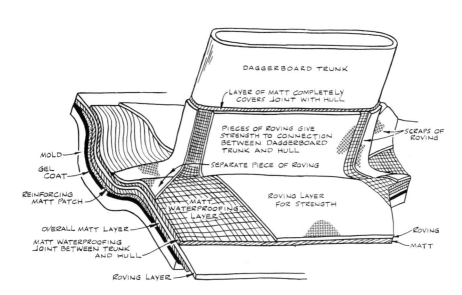

DAGGERBOARD TRUNK

LAYER OF MATT COMPLETELY
COVERS JOINT WITH HULL

PIECES OF ROVING GIVE
STRENGTH TO CONNECTION
BETWEEN DAGGERBOARD
TRUNK AND HULL

SCRAPS OF
ROVING

MOLD

GEL
COAT

SEPARATE PIECE OF ROVING

REINFORCING
MATT PATCH

MATT
WATERPROOFING
LAYER

ROVING LAYER
FOR STRENGTH

OVERALL MATT LAYER

ROVING

MATT WATERPROOFING
JOINT BETWEEN TRUNK
AND HULL

MATT

ROVING LAYER

FIGURE 2-38. *The daggerboard trunk attached to the hull.*

roving to the portion of the deck on either side of the cockpit where the people will be normally sitting, to give extra support to this area.

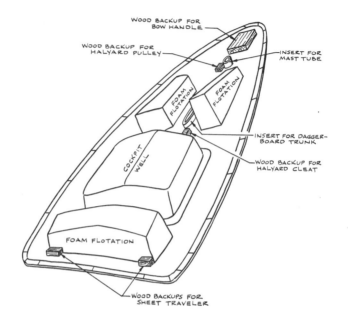

WOOD BACKUP FOR
BOW HANDLE

WOOD BACKUP FOR
HALYARD PULLEY

INSERT FOR
MAST TUBE

FOAM
FLOTATION

FOAM
FLOTATION

INSERT FOR DAGGER-
BOARD TRUNK

WOOD BACKUP FOR
HALYARD CLEAT

COCKPIT
WELL

FOAM FLOTATION

WOOD BACKUPS FOR
SHEET TRAVELER

FIGURE 2-39. *The underside of the deck when it is ready to be bonded to the hull.*

RUDDER FITTINGS

Figure 2-40 shows the two wood blocks which must be added to the back of the hull where the rudder will be attached. The rudder fittings are made of metal and will be attached to the boat with wood screws driven through the hull into the wood blocks. Because the rudder takes large stresses, these blocks must be attached securely. The small voids between the wood blocks and the hull are filled with a mixture of resin and microballoons (or sawdust). This filler will seal the joint between the wood block and the hull, preventing leaks from the screw holes required for the rudder fittings. Glass the wood blocks to the hull using a layer of matt followed by a layer or two of roving. Figure 2-37 shows these wood blocks in place in the rear of the hull.

MAST TUBE

If you study Figure 2-37 you will see that you must also install a mast tube. The mast tube can either be made on a mold, or it can be purchased as a fiberglass tube and sawed to the correct length on a bandsaw. Although the mast tube hole extends through the deck, it does not extend through the hull. The mast rests on the bottom of the hull when placed in the tube. Therefore, it is well to reinforce the area directly below the mast tube with an extra layer of roving before the tube is installed. When installing the tube, make sure that it is aligned correctly, so that it will match the hole already made in the deck. You will have to place the deck on top of the hull to check the alignment, and take measurements so that you can locate the tube properly when you remove the deck.

When attaching the tube to the hull, waterproof the joint between the bottom of the tube and the hull with a layer of matt all around. Then follow with strips of roving to securely anchor the tube to the hull. In use, the mast will be exerting tremendous pressure against the mast tube. You must use several layers of roving to connect the bottom of the tube to a large area of the hull, about a two-foot radius in size. When you have installed the two wood blocks in the stern, the daggerboard trunk, and the mast tube, the hull will be ready to be bonded to the deck.

DECK HARDWARE REINFORCEMENT

Several wood blocks must be added to the deck as shown in Figure 2-39. In the bow, a block must be glassed in to accept the screws which will hold the bow handle. Near the mast opening, there must be a small wood block to accept the screws taking the heavy load of the pulley which holds the halyard. This pulley takes more than just the weight of the sail plus the friction of the pulleys; it also must be able to take the surges of the sail and mast when the mast tries to rise out of the tube, as it will try to do under some conditions.

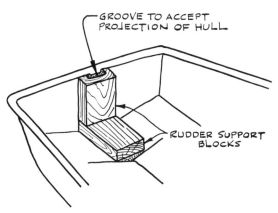

FIGURE 2-40. *Aft end of the hull ready to be assembled. Filler material must fill all voids under the rudder support blocks.*

Directly behind the slot for the daggerboard trunk there must be a wood block for the pulley which holds the sheet. Again, this pulley takes large strains during gusty wind conditions, and the wood block holding the screws which hold it must be glassed in firmly. At the rear of the deck are two wood blocks, one on each side, for the screws which hold the ends of the wire traveler rope. This wire rope holds the pulley which slides along it holding the sheet and must also be able to take the strains the sail imposes on it during gusts.

FOAM FLOTATION

In addition to the daggerboard trunk, the wood blocks, and the cockpit well, large pieces of foam must be added. Of course, all of these items must be positioned exactly so that there will be no hitches when the hull is placed on the deck. The foam needs to be cut to the correct shapes so that the hull will sit down on the deck, its flange touching the edge of the deck at all places.

PREPARING TO ASSEMBLE THE DECK TO THE HULL

Everything must be in readiness for rapidly assembling the hull and deck. Go through a "dry" run first to make sure that everything is positioned correctly, so that there will be no delays when finally assembling the hull and deck.

In this particular boat, it is important that there be a firm connection between the foam placed under the deck and the inside of the hull when the hull and deck are joined. To connect the foam to the deck, mix a little liquid foam, pour it on the deck where the foam is to be placed, and then quickly place the solid foam over the liquid foam, applying pressure. The liquid foam will almost immediately (within approximately 30 seconds) begin to expand. The pieces of foam must be held down over the expanding liquid foam for about a minute until the liquid foam has stopped rising. When this is done, the entire mass will be solid and will be attached to the deck moderately well.

When the hull is placed over the deck during the final assembly, you must pour small amounts of liquid foam on top of the pieces of solid foam where they will contact the hull. You will have to press down on the hull, keeping it firmly pressed against the deck until the liquid foam stops rising. After it stops rising, it will have connected the solid foam pieces to the hull, and will have filled any voids between the foam pieces and the hull. The foam becomes one solid piece between hull and deck, giving firm support to the deck. When a person walks on or sits on the deck, his weight is supported more equally by the hull because the foam transmits some of his weight from the flexible deck to the stiffer hull.

FIGURE 2-41. *Bonding the hull to the deck.*

Also some liquid foam should be poured under the cockpit where it touches the hull, and particularly where the drain plug will be inserted. The foam will once again transfer to the hull any weight placed on the floor of the cockpit well. It will also prevent leaks around the drain plug hole.

Also needed when the hull is assembled to the deck is a thick epoxy-glue filler where the mast tube joins the mast opening in the deck, and where the daggerboard trunk joins the daggerboard opening in the deck. The material should be very thick so it can prevent leaks as well as act as a bonding agent.

The third thing needed when assembling the hull to the deck is a method of bonding the flange of the hull to the edge of the deck. This is best achieved by putting thin strips of matt along the edge of the deck as shown in Figure 2-39. Just before finally assembling the hull to the deck, wet out the matt strips thoroughly so that they are quite soggy. When the hull is placed on top of the deck and the flange of the hull is tightly clamped to the edge of the deck, the wet matt will bond the flange of the hull to the edge of the deck. Figure 2-41 shows this step. Although only one clamp is shown in Figure 2-41, actually many, many clamps must be used so that they are spaced about every three inches.

ASSEMBLING THE DECK AND HULL

As you can perhaps imagine, the final step of actually assembling the boat is hectic to say the least. First you must spread epoxy resin on the mast tube and daggerboard trunk, and (to be safe) some on the mast and daggerboard openings in the deck. Then quickly you must wet out all the strips on the edges of the deck. Then you must measure out and mix the liquid foam, and quickly but accurately pour it on the pieces of foam and under the cockpit well. At this point, you need three or four helpers to put the hull quickly in place on the deck, in exactly the right place, so that the mast tube fits the opening in the deck and the daggerboard trunk fits into its opening. The foam pieces and cockpit all fit so that the flange fits tightly against the deck, the hull is straight on the deck, etc. You need to go through several dry runs ahead of the final assembly to be sure everything will fit perfectly.

After the epoxy resin, the polyester resin, and the liquid foam have been placed over the deck as in Figure 2-41, have your helpers sit on top of the hull for a minute or two until the foam has stopped rising. By sitting on the boat, they will prevent the foam from lifting the hull up off the deck. At the same time, they will be forcing the foam to flow all through the voids between the foam pieces and the hull, and the inside of the boat will partly fill.

As soon as the foam has stopped expanding, your helpers and you should immediately clamp up the flange all around. The entire assembly process to this point should take no more than 15 minutes, which is really moving unless you have many fellow workers. The epoxy resin which you used should be the type that takes much longer to set up than the polyester resin used on the matt strips. This will give you time to leisurely check the fit of the daggerboard trunk.

Since the boat is upside down, and the deck mold on which the entire assembly is resting is solid throughout (except the cockpit area), you cannot, at this time, check the fit of the mast tube in its opening in the deck. However, you can check the daggerboard trunk's fit by using a flashlight to look down the slot. If the trunk does not fit the deck slot correctly, stick a board in it and twist until it fits. Later when you remove the assembled boat from the deck mold, you can recheck the daggerboard trunk, and check the mast tube, adding epoxy resin to fill any holes which could cause a leak. To remove the assembled boat, of course, remove the C-clamps, and have someone help you lift the boat from the deck mold, being careful not to scratch it.

THE FINAL STEPS

First, you need to trim the edge of the boat where the hull meets the deck. Use a hacksaw, a hand circular saw with a special, thin grinding-wheel-type blade, or a sabre saw. If you use either type of power saw, make a jig that will guide the saw by holding it a set distance (about ¾″) from the side of the boat.

Beware! Put on a rubber raincoat, a hat, and otherwise cover your body with heavy clothing for this job if you use a power saw. The dust which is given off is extremely itchy and will annoy you greatly if it comes in contact with your skin. It is particularly annoying in such places as the inside of your elbows. The rubber raincoat and heavy clothing will reduce the amount of fiberglass dust which gets on you. Washing with strong soap, rubbing the wash rag in one direction only, helps to get rid of fiberglass dust sticking to your skin. The dust will not particularly harm you, but it will probably continue to annoy you for a couple of days.

Trimming the edge of the boat with a power saw and trimming the daggerboard trunk with a band saw creates a lot of dust. But if you trim the edge with a hacksaw, you will get less dust, a very sore arm, and probably a crooked edge.

The edge, after being trimmed, is best finished off with a lightweight, U-shaped molding made of either aluminum or plastic, riveted in place all along its length (rivets not farther apart than three or four feet). If you do not want to finish the edge this way, smooth it well with a file and sandpaper so it will not snag on your clothing or hands, and rivet it every two feet. Pop-rivets are fine for this job.

The fiberglass part of the job is now finished. You still have the accessories to make.

MAKING THE ACCESSORIES

Both the rudder and the daggerboard are made from wood. If you are making more than one boat from your mold, it is easier to make many rudders and daggerboards in one operation. This is done by using a router·and a pattern. For convenience, the router can be mounted under a table, with the rotating blade projecting through the table top. The pattern for the rudder or daggerboard is temporarily fastened to a piece of wood, which is then trimmed down to size. Finish the edges by sanding them. As you cut with the router, be careful to avoid catching a corner of the wood on the rotating rasp-like blade: it could grab the wood and pull your hand into it, giving you a severe cut. Naturally, you can cut the rudder and daggerboard to size with a coping saw or a sabre-saw if you do not have a router.

Figures 2-42 and 2-43 show the finished boat. You will probably want

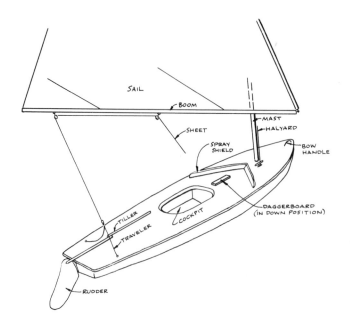

FIGURE 2-42. *Completed sailboard, deck view.*

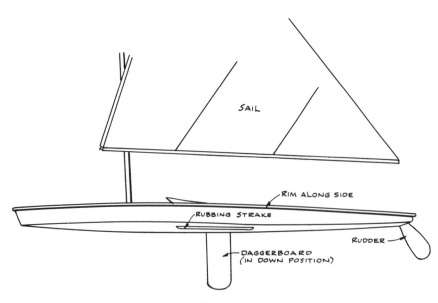

FIGURE 2-43. *Completed sailboard, profile view.*

to purchase an aluminum pipe from which you can make the mast and boom by adding the various fittings.

The finishing operation is not complete until you polish the entire boat with a fiberglass cleaner. If you keep the boat polished, it will retain its original gloss for many years.

The finishing operations, you will find, take almost as long as the entire building process.

CONCLUSION

What has been discussed is the actual building process used by one small-boat builder and is similar to that used by many small firms. This method of construction results in a well-made boat, and is quick if you already have the molds to work with. If you do not already have your own mold, you will have to make one to use this process. Making the mold is explained in the next chapter. You will find that making the mold and then a couple of boats using this method will probably be as fast as building a single wood boat.

3/ MAKING A MOLD FROM YOUR OWN DESIGN

You can make many things out of fiberglass, but first you must have a mold. To get a mold, you must build or borrow a prototype of the thing you want to build. In fiberglass work the prototype is called a *plug*.

Figures 3-1 and 3-2 help explain the relationship between a plug and a mold, and a mold and a finished part. As you can see, the plug or prototype is an exact duplicate of the thing you want to produce. In boatbuilding, it is often a perfectly finished wood boat. If the boat does not already exist, sometimes the prototype or plug is made from plaster.

Figure 3-1 shows the plug on the bottom in an upside-down position. The outside of the plug is shiny and flawless. The mold has been made over the plug, and the inside of the mold takes the gloss from the plug. In figure 3-1 the smooth glossy side of the mold is down, out of view.

Shown on the rough, upper surface of the mold are three legs. In Figure 3-2 the mold has been turned over and set down on the legs. Now the shiny side of the mold is up. The finished boat has been made in the shiny cavity of the mold (thus the name *cavity mold*). The finished boat is shown pulled out of the mold: the bottom is smooth and shiny, while the inside of the boat is rough.

It is possible to use an existing fiberglass boat as a plug to make another mold. As a matter of fact, this "stealing" of a design has occurred often. The usual tactic is to modify the boat just enough so that it is not identical to the original. However, not only is this method of obtaining a mold legally suspect, but also anybody who expects to sell a stolen design will be coming in on the short end: he will be selling a boat after the original manufacturer has already saturated the market with that kind of boat.

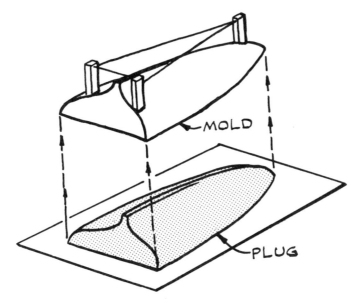

FIGURE 3-1. *Mold being pulled from a plug.*

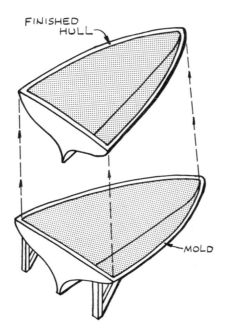

FIGURE 3-2. *Finished boat being pulled from a mold.*

A better method is to make a plug of an original design. The plug must be as perfect as possible, because the mold will pick up any defects the plug has, and it is difficult to work out such defects in the mold. And of course all parts coming out of the mold will mirror the defects of the mold.

What is the fastest and cheapest way to build a plug and then a mold for a new design? This is the topic of this chapter.

For a relatively small amount of money, you can build a plug for a pram or dinghy, make a mold, and build several boats, selling all but one to defray expenses. *It is strongly recommended that you start with a simple boat* in order to acquaint yourself with the techniques of working with fiberglass. Once you have accomplished this, the task of building a larger boat will be easier and faster.

MAKING THE PLUG FROM PLANS

You could build your new boat using conventional wood construction. When finished you would have a fine boat from which you could take a mold, and you could then either sell the boat or use it yourself. But this method is far more costly and time-consuming than the plaster mockup method. Quickly look at Figures 3-3 and 3-18 through 3-22 to get an idea of this method.

Briefly, the plaster mockup method involves building a flimsy wood and cardboard skeleton and filling it up with plaster, which is then smoothed off to provide the finished surface. This technique will save you time and money, particularly on designs that have rounded surfaces; conventional plywood construction should be used for designs that have mostly flat surfaces or simple (non-compound) curves.

The plaster-plug method, although potentially fast, inexpensive, and easy, requires careful attention to detail. It is not a foolproof method and can easily result in a mess. If you are skilled at woodworking, you might find it easier to build your prototype of wood, as applying plaster requires considerable experience before a good result can be achieved. But if you do choose plaster, be sure to do each step accurately. Skimping here and there might save money, but in the end it can be costly if you find that your project has several major flaws and must be done all over again.

For this example, let us assume you are going to build a 20-foot round-bilge sailboat. There are scores of plans available for this type of boat. Inexpensive plans can be bought from the International Amateur Boat Building Society, *Rudder, Popular Boating, Mechanix Illustrated,* Douglas Fir Plywood Association, and various plan and kit manufacturers. The point is that for any one type of boat, you can probably find at least

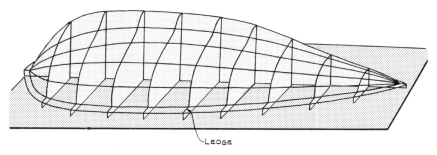

LEDGE

FIGURE 3-3. *Frame for building a plug. Note that each frame has a ledge for defining the sheer.*

a dozen good sets of plans almost identical in size and layout.

The plaster-plug method will be more successful the closer together the stations are located (see Figure 3-3). The very maximum the stations can be spaced is 18″ for reasonably good results, and it is desirable to have them as close together as six inches. When comparing competitive plans that are otherwise suitable, choose the one with stations more closely spaced together.

Many boat plans published today have full-size patterns and do not require lofting. However, if you have a design that requires lofting, you must draw the lines full size on a ⅛″ sheet (or sheets, as needed) of untempered masonite, which is cheaper than the outdoor type. Thin sheet metal, ¼″ masonite, or plywood may be substituted but are not recommended. Lay the lines out carefully, and double- and triple-check all measurements. If you do not know how to loft lines, refer to any number of books on wooden boatbuilding that explain lofting.

Very few boat plans call for locating the stations more closely than 16″ apart. This is too far apart for really good results — the ideal spacing is 6″. To bring the stations closer together, you will have to draw in additional stations between those already indicated. This additional drawing is done on top of the full-size drawings you have already made.

CUTTING OUT THE STATIONS

It is extremely important that you be accurate when cutting out the stations. You will probably want to use a sabre-saw for this job. Use a fine metal blade so that you can cut slowly and more accurately. You must have a steady hand and a good eye for this job, or you will have much agony later.

Place two pieces of ½″ or ⅝″ interior plywood (best side up) under the ⅛″ masonite template on which you have drawn the station lines. Line up the edges very carefully with the reference lines (see Figure 3-4). Clamp the two pieces of plywood and the template together tightly and make as smooth a cut as possible.

One by one, cut out the stations, working from the outermost lines first. By cutting the outermost ones first, you will avoid cutting across any of the other station lines you have drawn on the template (with the exception of the keel area — there you will have to save the scraps and piece them back together, as shown in Figures 3-4 through 3-8).

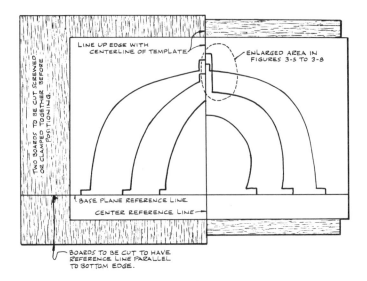

FIGURE 3-4. *Lining up the template with boards to be cut for the frames.*

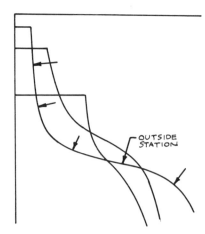

FIGURE 3-5. *An outside station cutting across inside ones near the keel.*

Incidentally, the purpose of using a template with all of the station lines down on it, rather than drawing the lines directly on the plywood to be cut, is to avoid mistakes and inaccuracies. By drawing the reference lines only once, there is no danger of their varying from station to station. Also, this method makes it easy to set up a reference plane (see Figure 3-4).

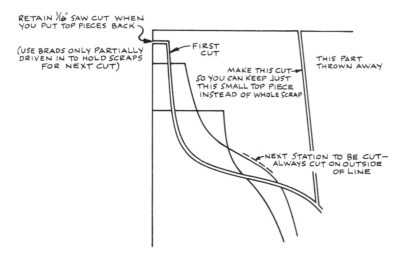

FIGURE 3-6. *Cutting out the first frame.*

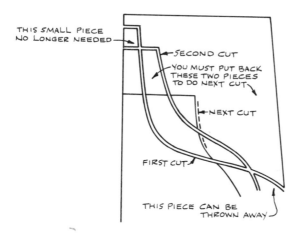

FIGURE 3-7. *Cutting out the second frame.*

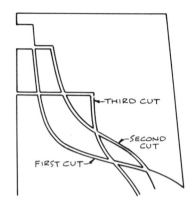

FIGURE 3-8. *Cutting of frames completed. The scraps can be discarded.*

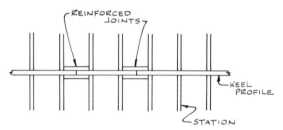

FIGURE 3-9. *Making a straight keel. Either space the stations or trim the keel profile so that the joints will fall between stations. Reinforce the joints with pieces of plywood.*

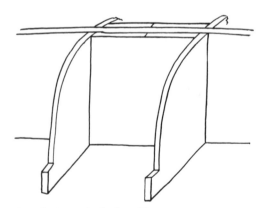

FIGURE 3-10. *Reinforced joint in the keel profile.*

MAKING THE KEEL PROFILE STATION

The keel profile should be drawn on several full sheets of ¾" plywood, rather than ⅛" masonite. All reference lines for placing the stations should be drawn on both sides of the keel frame. It will take several pieces of plywood for the entire keel, as it would be prohibitively expensive to buy oversize sheets in order to draw the keel profile on one sheet. Make certain the joints you make in the plywood fall halfway between frame station lines. The keel must be perfectly straight (see Figures 3-9 and 3-10). Cut out the keel with a saber-saw with a metal blade; do not bevel it at all.

MAKING THE BASE PLANE

It is very important that the plug be built on a level surface. If the floor you are working on is not level, construct a floor as shown in Figure 3-11. Once the floor is level, the base plane can be lightly constructed of single ½" plywood sheets. All reference lines are then drawn on the base plane.

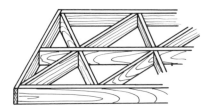

FIGURE 3-11. *Bracing for the base plane. Plywood is laid over this to make a deck.*

LINING UP THE STATIONS PROPERLY

In theory, the stations do not have any thickness and line up exactly on the station lines. However, the stations are actually made of ½" plywood.

In order to place a station properly on a station line, you must put it on one side or the other of the line. The side you pick will be determined by the keel profile — no part of the station should project beyond the keel profile line. Points A and B in Figure 3-12 indicate this clearly. Station 1 has been placed to the *right* of line 1; as shown at point A, the left side of station 1 just touches the juncture of line 1 and the keel profile line, and its right side is well below the profile line and out of the way. Station 5, however, is placed to the *left* of line 5. This is done so that the right edge of station 5 just touches the junction of line 5 and the keel profile line, and the left edge of station 5 does not jut above the profile line, as it would do if the left side of the station had been placed on station line 5.

ASSEMBLING AND FAIRING THE FRAME

You will need help in holding the large sheets of plywood used to make the frame, but assembling the frame should be fairly easy if you have been careful up to this point. Connect the stations to the keel and the base with corner irons, which can be salvaged later.

When the frame has been assembled, the form of the boat will be very obvious, and you will probably be dreaming of your cruise aboard her already. How much more work you have left on the plug will depend on how steady your hand was when you cut out the stations. The edges of the frames must be made smooth and must join the keel smoothly. Use a power sander until the edges are right, but go easy as the ⅛" edge is very delicate. Now paint the frame edges with polyester resin that has a wax additive, and when they are dry, sand them smooth. Keep sanding and repainting until the surface is very smooth.

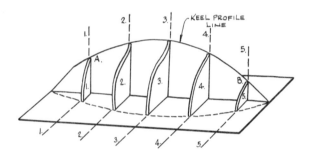

FIGURE 3-12. *Locating the frames.*

LAYING IN THE SHEER

On any object, certain lines are most crucial for the sake of appearance. On a boat hull, the outlines formed by the keel and the sheer are most important. At this point in the construction of a plug, the keel should be perfect. The sheer requires the same attention to detail.

As you can see in Figure 3-3, each frame has a small ledge that marks the location of the sheer. In theory, this sheer line could be built with the same plaster-batten method that is used for the rest of the plug. In practice, however, it is extremely difficult to get a perfectly smooth line at the sheer with plaster, so another construction method must be used. The answer is to build the sheer with continuous strips of molding that have been ripped into ¼" by ¼" strips. Molding, rather than less expensive wood, is specified because it is normally made of the best grade of wood.

These delicate stringers are glued to each station as shown in Figures 3-13 through 3-15. You could nail them, but the nail holes might cause splits, which would make the curve slightly untrue at each place the stringers are nailed. If the nail holes were predrilled, the stringers would be weakened and bend more sharply where they were drilled. To make the sheer one-inch wide, three more stringers are laminated to the first (see Figure 3-15). Now carefully sand these laminated strips and paint them with waxed polyester resin. Repaint and sand them smooth over and over, using a finer grit sandpaper each time, until the surface is very smooth.

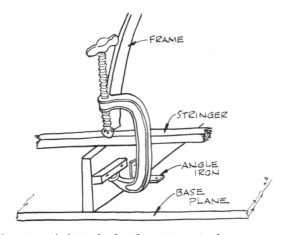

FIGURE 3-13. *Clamping and gluing the first sheer stringer in place.*

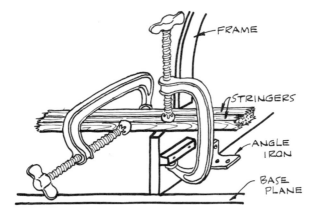

FIGURE 3-14. *Clamping and gluing the second sheer stringer in place.*

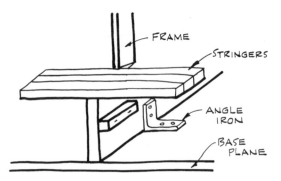

FIGURE 3-15. *All three sheer stringers in place.*

THE TRANSOM

Another part of any boat that is important from the appearance standpoint is the transom. Cut the transom from a piece of ⅛" masonite. If the exact shape of the transom is not shown on the plans, you may want to develop it by mechanical drawing methods. See Chappelle's book, *Boatbuilding*, for a detailed explanation. Another fairly acceptable method for drawing the transom is to hold a sheet of masonite in place at the stern of the mockup and have someone trace the line the end of a batten indicates when moved along the last few stations at the stern (see Figure 3-16).

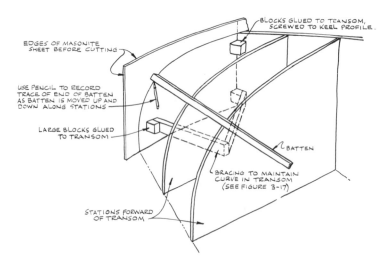

FIGURE 3-16. *Tracing and attaching the transom to the frame assembly.*

ADDING BRACING FOR PLASTER

When you have the transom cut out, attach it, fastening it first to the keel and then to the base plane with angle irons or small wood blocks (see Figures 3-16 and 3-17). Now paint it with waxed polyester resin and sand smooth. Repaint and keep sanding it until it is very smooth.

You must now add bracing composed of stringers and cardboard or screening as shown in Figures 3-18 through 3-20. This job does not have to be neat; however it must be (1) strong enough to hold the plaster to follow, (2) added gently so you do not throw the frame out of line, and (3) put in so that no portion comes closer than ⅛″ to the final surface (ideal if all of it is exactly ⅛″ from the final surface).

Now cover the stringers with scraps of cardboard, screening, masonite, heavy cloth, or anything which will be strong enough to hold the wet plaster until it sets. The purpose of the covered bracing is to keep you from needlessly filling the entire space between frames with plaster.

Probably the battens you used to draw the lines will do fine for smoothing the plaster. They should be smooth, long enough to cover at least six frames, and fairly easy to hold. Battens about the size and shape of a yardstick will do well. Also, a metal rule may work. As you work the plaster, if you are using a wood batten, you will damage the batten quickly unless it is painted. A good paint for this purpose is waxed polyester resin, because it is tough. Paint and sand half a dozen good battens of varying sizes (different cross-sections). See Figure 3-22.

Finally you are ready to begin plastering. The difficult part is still in front of you. If you are a reasonably adept woodworker, you should have accomplished this much quite quickly, considerably faster than if you were building a wood boat using conventional methods. The plastering also goes fast once you have practiced a little.

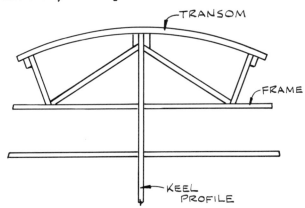

FIGURE 3-17. · *Transom assembly (looking down on it).*

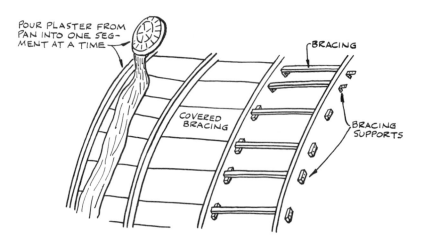

FIGURE 3-18. *Adding the bracing between frames. The bracing can be supported with either wood blocks or angle irons and then covered with cardboard, masonite, plywood, or screening.*

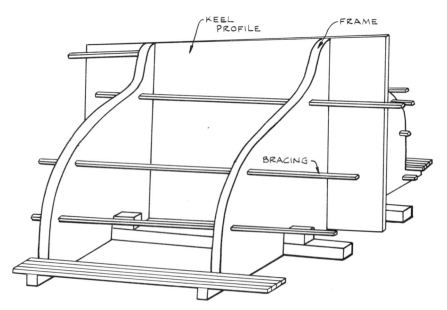

FIGURE 3-19. *Frame detail with bracing in place. The base plane is not shown.*

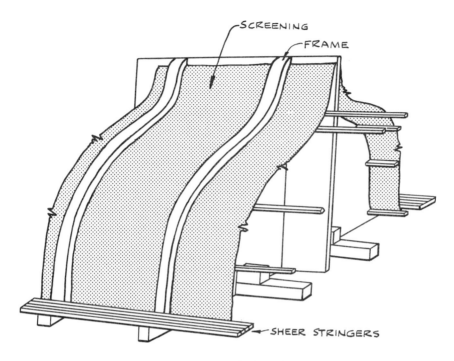

FIGURE 3-20. *Frame detail with screening applied over bracing.*

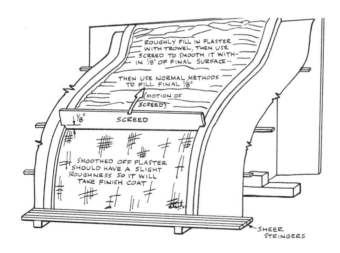

FIGURE 3-21. *Frame detail with plaster being applied. This method is used if the bracing has been put in deeper than ⅛" from the finished surface.*

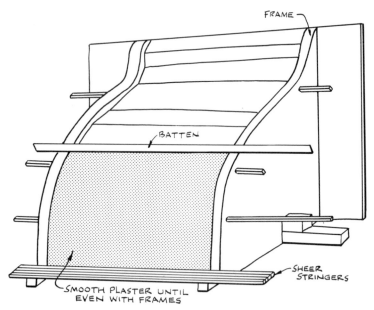

FRAME

BATTEN

SHEER STRINGERS

SMOOTH PLASTER UNTIL EVEN WITH FRAMES

FIGURE 3-22. *Frame detail with the final surface being faired. The flexible batten should be stretched across as many frames as possible to remove the uneveness of the plaster.*

MIXING THE PLASTER

The most economical filler for the plug is molding plaster. If cost is not a prime consideration, though, you may substitute a polyester auto body repair filler for plaster. It will not harden as quickly as plaster and will sand more easily when dry.

If you use molding plaster, it is important that you mix it properly. The way it should be mixed may at first seem unduly slow and exacting, but you will get a perfect mix every time. When you hurry and mix the plaster the way you always thought it was done, you will get it either too thin or too thick and lumpy. Haste makes waste. Do everything just as specified and you will be done faster than you think.

Use a wash basin to mix the plaster. This will give you just a small amount of plaster at a time, but that is enough. A small amount is all you can effectively spread with the batten at one time. Also the plaster sets up extremely fast, making a small amount all you can use at one time.

Fill the basin one-half full with cool, clean water. With your hand or a small cup, scoop up some plaster and sprinkle, not dump, it into the water. Move your hand around to sprinkle it all over the entire surface of the water. By sprinkling it, all of the plaster will get some water on it, which means you will not have to mix the plaster very much. Also, you will avoid lumps. If you throw the plaster in, you will get many lumps, which will make bad spots in the plaster. Lumps are areas of plaster which do not have enough water for complete hydration and therefore are too soft and crumbly when the plaster sets up.

As you sprinkle, the plaster will settle to the bottom. Keep sprinkling, cup after cup, until the plaster comes up to the surface of the water. By sprinkling over the entire surface of the water, the plaster will surface all over the entire pan at once.

When the plaster is touching the surface all over the pan, then it is time to mix. Once mixed, the plaster will set up rapidly (a couple minutes). But you can postpone mixing at this point, and it will not set up for a much longer time (as much as a half hour). To mix, immerse your hand completely in up to the wrist and mix. Then rinse your hand in a pail of water. Never wash in a sink as the plaster will clog the drain.

APPLYING THE PLASTER

Quickly pour the contents of the pan on a surface that is fairly flat. It is best to work one or two segments at a time, rather than having the plaster spill over into other segments as you pull the plaster with the batten.

After pouring the plaster (see Figures 3-18 and 3-21) with an assistant helping, pull the batten over it. One pass often is sufficient to do the job, though sometimes a second or third pass is needed. More than that is seldom required. Make the second pass from the other direction. The first time over often will leave small crater-like holes. This is normal, especially if you were in a hurry when mixing and got lumps or dirt in the plaster. If you always mix the plaster as specified, you will get a minimum of these defects. See Figure 3-22.

You must hold the batten so your fingers do not drag in the plaster. Hold it perpendicular to the frames, or at least as perpendicular as possible. (This is particularly important near the bow. At the very point of the bow, one end of the batten will be held stationary at the point of the bow, while the other end is swept up or down.) Also place your hands on the batten immediately over the top of the station frames. The idea is to hold the batten tightly against the frames, but not so tightly as to dent the little ⅛" edge, nor so tightly that the batten cannot assume its natural curve between frames.

Pouring the plaster and passing the batten will normally take only a couple of minutes per batch of plaster. At the end of the cycle, one person should immediately clean the batten and wash basin, using paper towels, a sponge, and a large container filled with water. The other person should clean up any drippings of plaster that might stick out above the finished surface. Actually, it is best to clean up all drippings on the plaster, because it is difficult to determine which stick up above the finished surface without passing the batten over; and you do not want to do that again, since it will disturb the plaster that has just been poured and smoothed.

You must always remove any plaster that has hardened above the finished surface, so that the batten will not hit it on a later pass. If it were to hit such a hardened high spot, the batten would deflect up and leave a ripple (see Figures 3-23 through 3-25). It is best to have several assistants, if possible, to wash basins and mix the plaster while you and your helpers wield the batten. It is good for two or three people to man the batten, getting into position before the plaster is poured. Someone else, if possible, should pour the plaster. The faster you pass over the plaster, the more likely it is that you will get a perfect surface with just one pass. You will find this work exacting although not physically strenuous.

Mixing the plaster the way specified will give you a moderately thin mix. When trying to cover the sides of the plug that are nearly vertical, you might find that the plaster will run down onto the floor. If this should occur, mix the plaster as specified, but wait a few minutes until the plaster begins to harden, then quickly spread it. This requires split-second timing and very agile batten men. Do not under any circumstances mix more plaster into the water than is called for, as this will result in a weak and crumbly mix.

Each of the batches, though small, should cover an area about two feet square, if the bridging was put close to the finished surface as suggested. Do not follow with the next batch near the same spot until the first batch is hard, since the batten may scrape the first batch and damage it if still soft. Rather, use the second batch at the other end of the boat (or on the other side), and keep alternating batches end-for-end or side-for-side. That way, earlier batches will be hard when you return to nearby sections.

When you have finished this long and difficult task, there will undoubtedly be some small imperfections. Fill in pits with a small amount of plaster, and use the batten to smooth off. Avoid building up additional layers of thin plaster over good sections already laid down. Use a scraper (putty knife or plaster knife) to knock down any local high spots. Also a wood rasp used gently will remove high spots.

Putting on the plaster will undoubtedly take longer than one day. If it is your first job, it may take you a long time indeed until you are used to handling the batten. To preserve overnight the plaster which has been put on the plug, soak it with ample quantities of water applied with a soft sponge. Be careful not to damage the surface by rubbing. Just pat the wet sponge on the surface. If you allow the plaster to dry out too rapidly, it may crack. Also any new plaster which you put over it will be difficult to handle because the old, dry plaster will suck the water out of the new plaster.

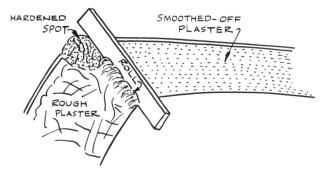

FIGURE 3-23. *High spot of hardened plaster forcing batten up. A roll of plaster has formed in front of the batten.*

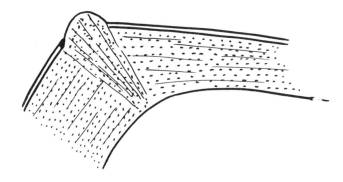

FIGURE 3-24. *Ripple in finished surface caused by the high spot illustrated in Figure 3-23.*

FIGURE 3-25. *Crown in finished surface caused by the bending of the batten under the weight of the plaster. A crown can also occur when the batten is held incorrectly.*

When you think you are done, stand back and examine the plug. If the job has been done correctly, the whole plug should be rather smooth, and all curves should be fair. If there are really serious problems, you can either chalk it up to experience and start over, or decide to build a boat with bumps. If you have only very minor problems, you will have to add plaster here and there, and scrape the areas smooth with the batten as best possible, until you are satisfied. This will be difficult because it will involve guesswork. But if you have followed the instructions carefully all along, you should have a perfectly acceptable plug that you can show your family and friends with pride.

When the plastering has been completed, allow the plaster to dry. During the first few days, sprinkle the surface a couple of times each day with water to prevent the surface from drying too fast and cracking. If the plaster should crack, wet the area around the cracks until they close. It may take a week for the plaster to dry thoroughly. When dry, it is ready for painting and final smoothing.

PAINTING AND FINAL SMOOTHING

Paint the plaster plug with acrylic lacquer primer, which is available in automotive supply stores. It is best to spray it on from the start. As it comes from the can, the primer is too thick to spray, and must be thinned about two parts of acrylic lacquer thinner to one part of primer by volume.

After several coats, the plaster should be fairly well filled in. There probably will be some high spots from slight irregularities in the surface of the plaster. This is the time to carefully remove them by sanding the entire surface.

It is debatable whether or not a power sander will really help you in the long run. A powerful orbital sander will help you achieve fast results; however, it is difficult to control, and you may wind up putting in irregularities, which will show up as wavy sections. If you do use a sander, it is important to keep the sander moving so that it does not bear down on any one place too long. In order to minimize gouging, hold the long axis parallel to the keel, and move it up and down around the boat rather than in a fore and aft direction. You may find that you will make as good progress using a large sanding block. Either way, these first couple of sandings will very quickly clog the paper up because you will break through the primer to raw plaster here and there.

As soon as you have broken through to raw plaster to any extent at all, spray on another coat of primer. It is important not to keep sanding when you have broken through to raw plaster, because the sandpaper will continue to dig out the raw plaster, while not bringing down the painted portions as quickly. You might produce a deep hole.

This is a long and tedious process, sanding and spraying, sanding and spraying, etc., until you have a surface which can be sanded without breaking through to raw plaster.

FILLING IN SMALL IRREGULARITIES

At this point you will want to fill in all the small irregularities and pinholes with putty. The proper type to use is either an epoxy two-part compound, a polyester two-part filler, or a one-part lacquer putty which dries by evaporation. Purchase these from an automotive supply store, and ask the clerk for one that is compatible with acrylic lacquers.

After the putty hardens, you will sand it, perhaps fill again, sand, and then spray another layer of primer. Of course you will want to go to finer sandpapers as you begin to get a very smooth surface, probably a no. 100 in an aluminum oxide or other nonclog sandpaper.

WET SANDING THE FINAL COATS OF LACQUER

After all the filling is done, spray on several layers of glossy black lacquer, wet-sanding between layers, until you finally have an extremely high-gloss surface with no visible irregularities or pinholes. These final wet sandings should be with progressively finer grades, starting with no. 320, then no. 400, and finally with no. 600 for the last coats. These last sandings should preferably be done by hand, as any kind of power sander tends to leave small scratches. Use a sanding block wherever possible, and move the sandpaper in one direction only.

When wet sanding use the following technique: Use a sponge to flow a small puddle of water under the sandpaper. The water will wash out sanding dust, keeping the sandpaper unclogged. On a sloping surface, place the sponge above the sandpaper, and keep a small amount of pressure on the sponge to produce a trickle of water flowing around the sandpaper at all times. Mop up the water which collects below the sandpaper from time to time. Avoid too much water as it is not necessary; use only enough to keep the sanding dust flushed out of the paper.

A wet-sanded surface is not glossy. All small pits are easily visible (after you dry the surface) because the paint in the pits is still glossy, and shows up against the dull surface where you have been sanding. At this point, any pits should be so small that putty will not stick in them. The only way to get rid of them is to continue spraying coats of paint and sanding them carefully until finally the pits are all gone, or at least your patience runs out.

You will notice when you sand with no. 600 wet-or-dry paper that, unlike no. 400, the surface begins to take on a dull gloss. This is because the surface is so smooth that it is beginning to take a shine.

Next use a polishing compound that can be obtained at an automotive supply store. If it comes in two grades, use the coarser first. Shake well to distribute the fine grit throughout the thick liquid. Apply a few dabs on the surface with a rag. Before it dries, buff it with a buffing pad placed over the grinding disc of a buffer-grinder (speed about 2,000 rpm). Move the buffer back and forth under light pressure (primarily the buffer's own weight).

Wipe off any dried residue with a clean rag. Clean the buffing pad by removing it from the grinder and slapping it against something. Wash and dry it between the two polishings if you are using medium and fine grades of polishing compound. When you finish polishing with the fine compound, you should have a uniformly high gloss.

You must be very careful when using a power buffer not to allow any part of the body of the buffer to touch the shiny surface in order to avoid scratches. Similarly, do not allow the temperature between the rotating pad and the surface to get so hot as to cause the compound to cake, or to scorch the surface. Avoid getting dust or other abrasives under the pad, as they can put in numerous small scratches.

A powerful buffer is a fairly dangerous tool to use. Be extremely careful not to allow the power cord to get caught in the rapidly turning buffing wheel. If it gets caught in the wheel it can break the cord, causing the machine to touch the "hot" broken ends and give you a shock or kill you. Or it could wrench your arm. And if it does no damage to you, it almost for certain will be pulled from your hand and will fall on the polished surface, putting.a deep scratch in it as it spins wildly before you can pull the plug. It takes hours of work to repair such scratches properly, and often they will not be completely repairable. So be very careful — keep your mind on the cord at all times — take the time to stop and move it out of the way as you move along.

MAKING THE MOLD FROM THE PLUG

Making the mold from the plug is very similar to making the finished part from the mold, which is described in great detail in Chapter 2. To summarize, you first wax the plug to a high gloss so the mold will separate from the plug when you later pull it off. Then spray a layer of PVA to doubly insure proper separation and spray gel coat on the plug. The gel coat used is called by some manufacturers "tooling gel coat," indicating that it is a tougher (and more expensive) gel coat especially suited for molds. Use either black or bright orange color, bright orange being preferred somewhat. The reason for using these colors is that they are not often used for boats. When you later spray up a boat in your mold, you will want the color you are spraying to contrast with the color of the mold so that you can see where you have sprayed and what still needs to be sprayed.

After the tooling gel coat hardens, follow it with a layer of matt, working out all air bubbles with as much or more care as described for the construction of a boat. Follow with enough layers of roving and matt to make the mold very stiff and strong. The construction of the mold must be much more substantial than that of the parts you will pull from it. This is because it is of utmost importance that the mold not flex or sag out of shape, because if it does, each part you pull will also be out of shape. As you can see, making the mold correctly is important because what you do here will determine what you will be making from it.

If the mold is large, you may want to use lightweight core material to make a sandwich construction to add great stiffness to the mold without making it extremely heavy. See Chapter 4 for a detailed description of how block balsa core material is used in making decks of large cruisers, for the same method would be followed if you use balsa to reinforce your mold.

Figure 3-26 shows the completed mold for a hull with a wood framework indicated above it. This wood framework is attached to the mold by glassing it with numerous fiberglass patches as shown in Figure 3-28. For light molds, an old ladder will provide a good frame to which you can add legs. The resulting frame should extend beyond each end somewhat so that you can lift it, with a person at each end. Adjust the heights so that you can reach the middle of the mold without touching the rim with your shirt as you lean over. You may wish to put wheels on the legs of the frame so that you can easily roll the mold out of your shop. If the mold is deep and difficult to reach into, you may want to fix the frame so that the mold can be tilted to each side easily by loosening and tightening a wing-nut fastening.

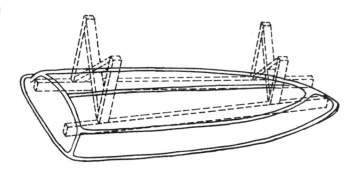

FIGURE 3-26. *Mold frame.*

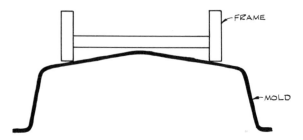

FIGURE 3-27. *Cross-section of the mold frame.*

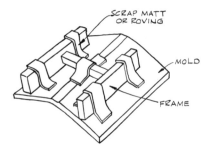

FIGURE 3-28. *Detail showing the method of attaching the frame to the mold.*

MAKING A MOLD FROM AN EXISTING BOAT

If you already have a copy of the boat you want to build in fiberglass, and it is in good condition, you will probably use it as a plug. This will save you the trouble of going through the complicated procedure just described to translate a set of plans into a plug.

The final surface of the boat must be made as smooth and glossy as you can get it. This means work if the boat has been in use long. You must fill all dents, paint, sand, repaint, sand again, etc., until the finish is almost like a mirror. But there are often some special problems which must be solved before proceeding to the sanding and painting stages. These problems are illustrated in Figures 3-29 through 3-46.

STIFFENING CONSIDERATIONS

Wood and fiberglass are different materials, with different structural properties. Because of the way wood is manufactured, many wood boats have large, flat areas such as those of the small rowing boat shown in Figure 3-29. This little boat, which has been made of plywood, has a perfectly flat bottom, flat sides, and sharp corners. The rub strakes on the

114

bottom have been rounded somewhat, but their corners are relatively sharp nevertheless. This sharpness and flatness is easy to achieve in wood construction, and because wood is quite stiff for its weight, the flat bottom and sides remain strong and stiff.

Figure 3-30 shows what is closer to the ideal shape for a fiberglass boat. Nowhere is there a flat area, and there are no sharp corners. From Chapter 2 on making small fiberglass boats, you know that you do not want to have sharp corners in fiberglass boats, because sharp corners are difficult to make without air bubbles. For practical considerations, sharp corners are ruled out. Flat areas are ruled out for a different reason: fiberglass is not as stiff as wood of the same thickness. To get the flat bottom of a fiberglass boat as stiff as a wood boat's, you would need to make the fiberglass twice as thick as normal, which would weigh too much, take too much material, and cost too much.

The nicely rounded shape of Figure 3-30 is good for fiberglass construction, and the flat, sharp-cornered shape of Figure 3-29 is good for wood construction. But you like your wood rowboat and think you could make money selling fiberglass replicas of it. What do you do? You could round off your wood boat as shown by the dotted lines of Figure 3-29. But this would be like building a new boat, and if you decide to do this, you would be wise to use the plaster mock-up method described earlier rather than ruining your good old rowboat.

FIGURE 3-29. *Ideal shape of a boat made of fiberglass.*

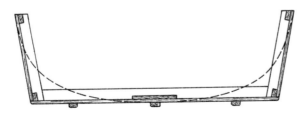

FIGURE 3-30. *Cross-section of a typical plywood boat. The dotted line shows the ideal shape of a fiberglass boat.*

Your best solution is to compromise. Figures 3-31 through 3-33 show how. Round off the sharp corners generously as shown in Figure 3-31. Add filler or quarter-round concave molding along the rub strakes; also add a ledge at the sheer, rounding the junction between the side and the ledge as shown in Figure 3-31. Now paint and sand to get your glossy, smooth plug, and make a mold from it. Figure 3-33 shows the outer shape of the boat you will make from it.

Although the modification of the old rowboat shown in Figure 3-29 eliminated the troublesome sharp corners, it did not eliminate the problem of the flat bottom and flat sides, and you will find that they will flex much too much when made in fiberglass of a reasonable thickness. You could at this point turn to sandwich construction, but you will probably find this is more expensive than you wish. If you were to run through a cost analysis on a small boat like this, you would find that the use of balsa core material raises the cost of construction excessively. Balsa core construction is suitable for large boats, but for small boats you can get all the added stiffness you need without resorting to the use of an expensive sandwich material.

Instead of using balsa, glass in some 2 x 2's as shown in Figure 3-33 in the three depressed areas formed by the rub strakes in the original plug. As you can see in the drawing, a layer of roving was placed across the entire bottom of the boat after the wood pieces were put in. Although the extra strength this improved construction will have is derived somewhat from the wood which has been molded in, most of the added strength results from the small girders which you have formed out of the fiberglass surrounding each piece of wood. This method of stiffening the bottom will be cheaper than using a balsa core, and will be stiff enough for a rowboat. (If you used the balsa, it would be extremely stiff, more than you need.) If you wish, mailing tubes can be substituted for the 2 x 2 wood strips and actually are better, because they are lighter and will bend with the fiberglass as it flexes.

Figure 3-33 shows a fiberglass flange built into the side of the boat at the gunwale. This flange does wonders for the flat side of the boat; it makes the side much stiffer. In order to beautify this flange, and add some strength to it as well, attach molding along the edges, as shown in Figure 3-33. If you do not like the idea of the little flange sticking out, then finish the edge as shown in Figure 3-32, which will also give the side the required stiffness and make it look nice and feel nice as well. You can finish an edge to be smooth, but it is difficult, and it is much more satisfactory to enclose it in a molding of some sort, or cover it up with wood. That way, no hands will get scratched on a stray, murderously sharp, glass fiber.

Figures 3-34 through 3-41 show various ways to modify a small boat with a flat deck for fiberglass construction.

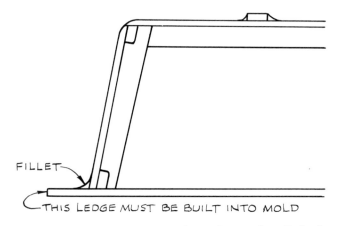

FILLET

THIS LEDGE MUST BE BUILT INTO MOLD

FIGURE 3-31. *Rounded-off corner on boat to be used as a plug. If the boat is to be finished with a molding as in Figure 3-33, a fillet as shown should be added.*

FIGURE 3-32. *Detail of wood molding at the sheer.*

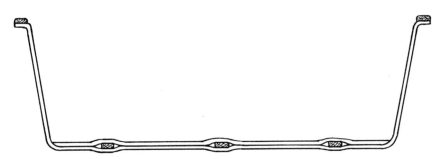

FIGURE 3-33. *One way to adapt the boat in figure 3-30 for fiberglass construction.*

117

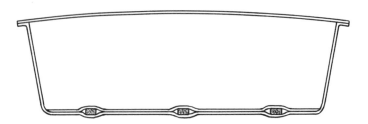

FIGURE 3-34. *Less desirable way to connect a curved deck to the hull.*

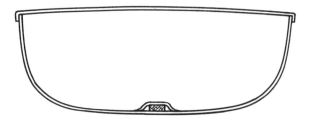

FIGURE 3-35. *Desirable way to connect a curved deck to the hull.*

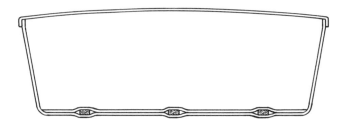

FIGURE 3-36. *Desirable way to connect a curved deck to the hull.*

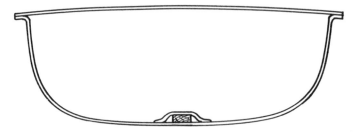

FIGURE 3-37. *Less desirable way to connect a curved deck to the hull.*

FIGURE 3-38. *Desirable way to connect a flat deck to the hull.*

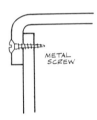

FIGURE 3-39. *Detail of the deck-to-hull connection used in Figures 3-35, 3-36, and 3-38.*

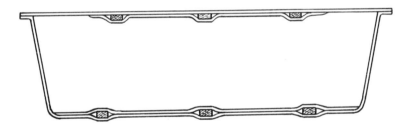

FIGURE 3-40. *Less desirable way to connect a flat deck to the hull.*

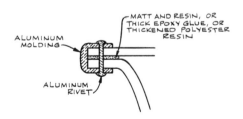

FIGURE 3-41. *Detail of the deck-to-hull connection used in Figures 3-34, 3-37, and 3-40.*

119

If you modified your rowboat to make it a round hull as shown in Figure 3-30, then you undoubtedly will want to round the deck also. Two different ways of attaching the deck to the hull are shown in Figures 3-35 and 3-37. Notice that I have indicated a wood piece glassed in the bottom of these hulls to give some extra stiffness. This might or might not be needed in the actual fiberglass boat, and you would have to determine it by test.

If you want to retain a flat deck just like the flat bottom and sides, you can make it out of fiberglass as shown in Figures 3-38 and 3-40. You will have to glass in some wood beams along the length of the deck as shown. Figure 3-38 shows the preferred method of attaching the deck to the hull (see also Figure 3-34). Figure 3-40 shows the easier way of attaching the deck to the hull, using a molding as shown in Figure 3-41.

Reverse Curves

But you may not be out of the woods yet. Look near the bow of your old rowboat. Do the sides possibly curve in toward one another? If they do, you will not be able to pull the finished part from the mold. In fact you will run into trouble long before that: you will not be able to get the mold off the plug. This reverse curve occurs in almost every canoe, and in many other boats as well. A curve shape has been used in Figures 3-42 through 3-46. When you have a shape such as this, you will have to either make your boat in two pieces or make your mold in two pieces. Let's talk about making the mold in two pieces first.

It should be obvious from examining Figure 3-42 that you could not pull out the finished canoe from the mold if the mold were all one piece. Therefore the mold is split down the middle, and bolted together as shown. When you have finished molding the canoe, unbolt the two halves of the mold and remove the part. Because the bottom of the canoe illustrated is flat, you will have to add a piece of wood along the inside of the bottom and glass it over for added stiffness. To get enough stiffness in the edges of the canoe, you will have to add molding along the edges, as shown in Figure 3-42.

The other way of making the same canoe is illustrated in Figures 3-44 through 3-46. Here, two separate molds are used, which enable you to make each half separately. Flanges must be molded as shown and bolted or riveted together to complete the canoe. If you use this method, you will not have to add stiffening inside the boat, as the riveted flanges will provide adequate stiffness along the bottom. Also, you will appreciate sitting on a smooth bottom instead of a lump when using the boat. But like everything else, there are disadvantages to the two-mold method of construction: the flange is a potential source of leaks, will cause the boat to draw more water than one with a perfectly flat bottom, and may hinder the maneuverability of the canoe.

120

FIGURE 3-42. *Cross-section of a canoe, a shape that cannot be pulled out of a single mold.*

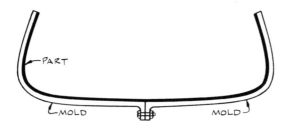

FIGURE 3-43. *A two-section mold that can be unbolted to remove the finished boat.*

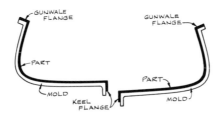

FIGURE 3-44. *The two-mold method of building a boat. After the halves have been pulled from the molds, they are connected along the keel flange.*

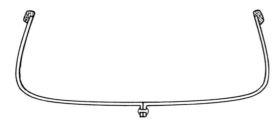

FIGURE 3-45. *A two-mold boat without gunwale flanges.*

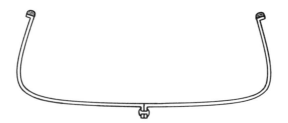

FIGURE 3-46. *A two-mold boat with gunwale flanges.*

The upper edge of the canoe on either side will have to be stiffened with molding as shown in Figure 3-45. Or if you build a little flange at this edge, you will get built-in stiffness all along the edge. Add a molding on top of this flange for beauty and protection (see Figure 3-46).

Making the mold shown in Figures 3-43 and 3-44 from the plug requires that you add a temporary ledge longitudinally along the centerline of the boat. If you plan to use the two halves of the mold together, as shown in Figure 3-43, make the junction of the bottom and the temporary ledge a sharp corner so that there will be only a fine crack between the two halves of the mold when bolted together. If you plan to use the two halves of the mold apart as shown in Figure 3-44, make the corner rounded a little, to ease the problem the corner will make when molding the part. The sharp corners making up the flange will be difficult to keep free of bubbles, requiring extra care when the flange is molded.

These considerations should enable you to tackle any existing boat with success when modifying it for fiberglass construction. Remember to avoid sharp corners and flat areas (especially large flat areas); and if you must keep flat areas, reinforce them by glassing in a wood member underneath. The curve throughout a formerly flat area need not be exaggerated as in the drawings: a slight curve will add a lot of strength to a fiberglass part.

FIGURE 3-47. *Hull with a straight edge.*

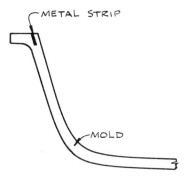

FIGURE 3-48. *Mold used to form a hull with a straight edge. An optional metal strip can be inserted to protect the mold when the straight edge is trimmed and sanded.*

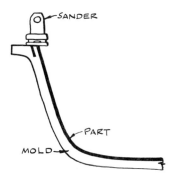

FIGURE 3-49. *Use of a sander to smooth the edge while the hull is in the mold.*

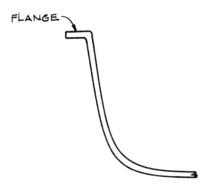

FIGURE 3-50. *Hull with a flange edge.*

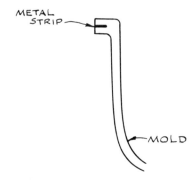

FIGURE 3-51. *Mold used to form a hull with a flange edge.*

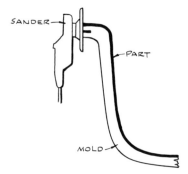

FIGURE 3-52. *Use of a sander to smooth the flange edge while the hull is in the mold.*

PREPARING AND MAINTAINING THE MOLD

After you have put on enough layers of fiberglass over the gel coat to make a strong mold, pull it off the plug. Sometimes a mold cannot be removed from the plug easily, although there are no reverse curves. This is also true of parts sometimes when you go to pull them from the mold. Therefore, it is wise to drill a small air hole someplace in the mold where it will not be conspicuous or where it will be cut away, as in a daggerboard slot. Compressed air can be forced into such a hole to help push the part from the mold, or the mold from the plug.

As you pull parts from the mold, you will have to wax thoroughly once between each part to maintain the gloss and to make certain each part separates easily. When needed, you should rebuff the entire mold again with compounds, and then rewax. By being careful about this, you will be able to use the mold many times over, realizing much profit from it. With care you should be able to get a minimum of fifty parts from it and perhaps up to 200.

Eventually a mold loses its gloss in spots from use. No matter what you do you cannot restore it in certain areas. If these areas are in critical spots, where they can be seen easily, you may have to discard the mold early. If the dull spot or spots are in out-of-the-way places, you may continue with the mold for a long time, as the dullness does not harm the structural quality of the boats pulled from the mold.

Also as a mold ages, cracks develop. If you have made the mold very strong, and have heavily reinforced it through the supporting frame, these cracks will be long in appearing. However, you probably will get cracks eventually. They occur particularly around areas involving sharp turns, such as the opening in the deck for the mast, the openings for the daggerboard and centerboard, or along the cockpit or edges. These cracks, which often occur in great numbers like fine spokes of a wheel all radiating from one spot, much like a piece of shattered safety glass, reproduce in great fidelity in the parts you pull from the mold. To the person who does not know where the fine lines came from in the finished boat, the cracks look like damage, whereas they actually do not affect the strength of the boat at all.

These cracks can be removed with some degree of success by a laborious process. You must drill out the source of the cracks perhaps 1/16" below the surface. Then drill similar holes at the other end of the cracks, and with a sharp tool scrape a gouge along as many cracks as you think you will have patience to refill and sand and polish to a high gloss.

Refill the shallow holes and gouges with tooling gel coat. Try your best to fill them only slightly above the surface of the mold, because gel coat is excruciatingly difficult to sand down. Place a piece of wax paper over the gel coat, sealing out all air so that it will harden tack-free. When it has hardened, break out the no. 400 wet-or-dry sandpaper, and wet-sand the gel coat until it is almost level with the surface of the mold. If you applied just the right amount of gel coat instead of large gobs of it, you will not have to sand for hours. Remember, all this is hand sanding — a sander would be too risky; you might put more scratches in the mold than you were trying to remove.

When you are very close to getting the gel coat patch down to the surface of the mold (you can tell by feel, and by close examination after wiping up the water you are using to do the wet sanding), then bring the gel coat to the exact level of the mold using no. 600 wet-or-dry sandpaper, wet sanding of course. After that is done, polish extensively in the area with medium compound, follow with fine compound, wax the area many times, wax the whole mold a couple of times for good measure, and probably you will have removed most of the cracks. Unless you are extremely skilled, your repair will not be invisible on the boats pulled from the mold. It will show as a slight unevenness, but will look much better than the cracks.

The pity of it all is that about four or five boats later the cracks will reappear. Eventually, when you get enough cracks and several dull spots thrown in as well, you will get tired of repairing the mold, throw it away, and make a new one. If you protected your plug carefully, you should be able to take another mold from it with little effort. If your plug did not make it, you can use one of your finished boats to make a mold from, waxing the boat well before spraying it up. Of course the boats you pull from this mold will not be quite as accurate in each dimension as the plug was or should have been, but it will not be something you will be able to see with the naked eye.

Sometimes, as you use a mold over again and again, the parts begin to stick. If one of the parts sticks hard and has to be ripped out, you stand a good chance of damaging the mold, as some of the gel coat of the part will stick to the mold, or some of the gel coat of the mold will stick to the part, or there will be numerous cracks where the sticking occurred. Always wax thoroughly between parts.

Of course sometimes you suspect that you are waxing too much, that the parts are sticking because of an excessive build-up of wax. So for a few parts you wax only once between parts, and all goes well. If you use the grinding compounds after every few parts pulled, you should have little difficulty from this problem, as the grinding compounds remove the wax, and the wax on the mold will always be relatively fresh. Often it is good to compound very carefully the entire mold at the first sign of a part beginning to stick. (Typically one part sticks just a little, the next alerts you to the impending problem, the third makes you cuss it out, the fourth gets you really worried, and the fifth ruins either the part or the mold).

Care of the mold is really important. Because of the heavy construction required of a good mold, a mold is quite expensive to make, often four to five times as expensive as the boat which will be made from it (which is not cheap). With real care, you will be able to pull from it many times the value of the materials which went into the mold.

One of the best protections you can give an unused mold is to leave a finished part in the mold unpulled. Since all parts stick in the mold at least a little bit, by not pulling the last part molded in it, you get a positive seal against dust and objects that might fall on the mold. When the mold is needed once again, you have a part all ready to go, and the mold will be in perfect condition.

4/ MAKING LARGE
FIBERGLASS BOATS

Making a large fiberglass boat is very similar to making a smaller one, such as the one described in Chapter 2. In this chapter, the construction of a large fiberglass power cruiser and a large fiberglass keel sailboat will be discussed. In addition, what few differences there are between the two will be covered.

A LARGE FIBERGLASS CRUISER

Figure 4-1 shows the mold for a large cruiser. As you can see, the mold must be heavily reinforced, much more so than for a small boat. The mold is enclosed in a framework of welded steel pipe, connected to the fiberglass mold by strips of fiberglass that loop around the pipes. Because it would be difficult to work inside such a large mold in the upright position, it is made to pivot to either side.

After spraying the mold, the first layer of reinforcment is applied to the portion which can be reached without walking inside the mold, and then allowed to cure. Then the workers walk on it to get to the remainder of the gel coat that requires the first layer of reinforcement. Sometimes special scaffolding is constructed to allow the men to reach all parts of the boat without walking inside the mold.

After the first layer is on and cured, the workmen walk inside the mold with shoes, being careful not to slip on any resin that may drip from the upper portion they are working on. The skeg is laid up first; as you can imagine, it takes a long arm to reach to the bottom of the skeg at the transom. The pieces of cloth and roving are cut roughly to shape beforehand, and stacked in rolls beside the work area.

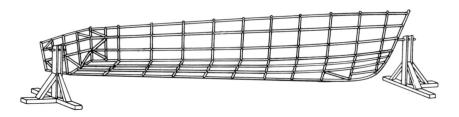

FIGURE 4-1. *Mold for a larger cruiser. The mold is reinforced with a welded steel pipe frame and pivoted at its ends so it can be turned to either side.*

In a cruiser of this size, there may be seven layers of roving in the bottom (making a total thickness of ⅜″ to ½″ and five layers on the side (about ¼″ thickness). The stern is reinforced with balsa core sandwich material, glassed over on both sides with several layers of matt and roving. The mold is pivoted to the other side next to enable the workers to finish it.

When working on a boat of this size, it makes sense to use a spray gun that mixes resin and activator in the gun just before it is sprayed out. This is in contrast to a normal spray gun, which requires that the activator be mixed into the resin before it is put into the tank. By having the resin mix with the activator in the nozzle, you use only the amount of resin you need, rather than having to shoot an entire batch of preactivated resin, as you have to do with normal spray equipment. Also, an acetone flush button, shown in Figure 4-2, makes it easy to clean the gun.

This rig has a pump and motor, tanks for activator and acetone, and a long extension arm to support the hoses going to the gun (to take the weight of the hoses off the arms of the operator). There are valves to regulate the amount of activator added to the resin. The entire outfit is on rollers so that it can be moved from mold to mold. A typical rig of this type may cost $1,000 to $2,000. Although costly, it pays for itself in a large operation by saving labor and by reducing materials waste.

Figure 4-3 shows the plywood reinforcing which is installed in the bottom of the hull while it is still inside the mold. These plywood forms are securely glassed to the hull and fastened to each other. They form a strong reinforcement for the bottom of the hull. In addition they provide a support for the flooring and cabin work to be added later. Before the floor is put in, the engines, propeller shafts, gas and water tanks, and generators are installed. The plywood forms are cut away where necessary to fit the machinery.

Figure 4-4 shows the deck mold for the hull shown in Figures 4-1 and 4-2. This mold does not pivot. Instead, platforms are built around it on which the workers stand. Most of the job, however, must be done

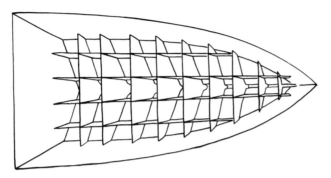

FIGURE 4-2. *Plywood forms fiberglassed into a hull to provide reinforcement. These forms also support flooring and serve as a mount for engines and other accessories.*

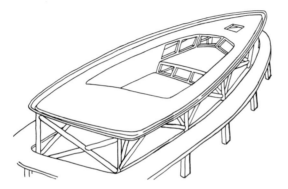

FIGURE 4-3. *Deck mold for a larger cruiser, with a platform for the workers.*

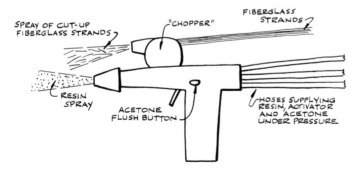

FIGURE 4-4. *Spray gun with chopper.*

inside the mold — the workers must walk in their stockinged feet and be very careful not to scratch the buffed and waxed mold. When putting on the various layers, the workers must work from the middle to the edges of the mold.

Figure 4-2 shows the spray gun which is part of the larger spray gun rig. The gun has an accessory mounted on it called a *chopper,* which cuts long fiberglass strands into short (¼") lengths and blows them onto the surface of the mold, where they are wetted by a spray of activated resin. The fiberglass strands are fed to the gun from a large spool. The chopper makes a loud, high-pitched noise when in operation.

After the gel coat has been sprayed and is firm, the chopper is used to cover the entire mold with a fairly thick layer of chopped strands. It is sprayed in sections starting near the middle. The men must scramble onto the mold and, using rollers, roll the wet strands into a compact layer, removing any air bubbles. Then another section is sprayed up, and the men quickly roll that out, until, section by section, the entire deck is covered with a layer of strands.

After this layer of chopped strands and resin has cured, balsa core material (see Figures 4-5 through 4-7) is installed. To do this, a second layer of chopped strands is shot on the area where the balsa is to be placed. The balsa is then pressed into the wet strands, with the loose fiberglass weave attached to the balsa facing down. When the resin has cured, the balsa will be securely glued to the deck. Incidentally, the interior of the cabin is bonded to the hull in the same manner — plywood or other finishing materials is imbedded in a freshly sprayed layer of strands.

The balsa core layer is sprayed again with chopped strands to cover the upper side of the balsa. This makes the entire construction into a type of girder as shown in Figure 4-6. This layer is also rolled out. Additional layers are added and rolled out as called for by the design.

You will notice that chopped strands are not used in the construction of the hull, only for the deck. Chopped strand construction is relatively heavy, weak, and brittle (because of the high amount of resin) and should not be used in the hull where high strength is needed. However, the strength of the deck is not as critical, so the chopped-strand method can be used instead of the hand-layup method. This will save labor costs.

A great deal of finish work goes into the construction of a large fiberglass cruiser. Finish work accounts for over half the time required to build an entire boat. Though some of the parts on the inside of the hull can be molded from fiberglass, most of the finishing work is done using the same materials as would be used to finish a wooden boat.

Before the deck is assembled in place on the hull, much of the interior of the hull is finished. The deck is lowered onto the hull by a crane. The hull has been pulled from its mold by this time and has been placed

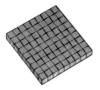

FIGURE 4-5. *Balsa core material. The blocks of end-grain balsa are held together by loosely weaved fiberglass.*

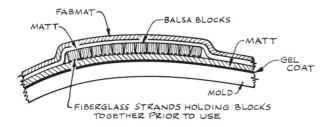

FIGURE 4-6. *Use of core material to stiffen fiberglass construction.*

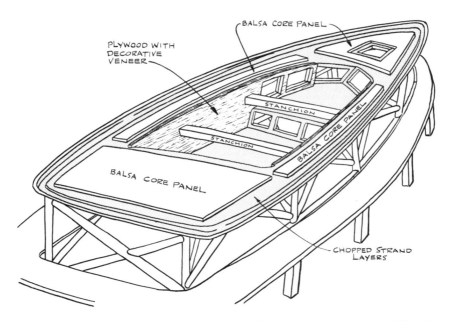

FIGURE 4-7. *Deck mold for a large cruiser with balsa core panels in place. The plywood panels are held in place with stanchions until the resin sets up.*

on a moveable dolly or trailer. The bottom of the hull must be sanded and painted with antifouling paint, the boot-topping and name put on, all outside fittings added, and all interior work finished. Access is gained to the inside of the boat by a ladder or by a moveable ladder-platform.

A LARGE FIBERGLASS SAILBOAT

The large fiberglass sailboat to be discussed in this section is one about 25 feet long with a keel. It is of such a shape that it is best to make the hull and deck from the same mold, rather than from separate molds as in the cruiser discussed previously (see Figures 4-8 and 4-9). The mold is split down the centerline, with each half of the boat molded separately (see Figures 4-10 and 4-11). Several layers of roving and matt are used to make the hull about ½" thick and the deck about ⅜" thick. The chopped strand method is not used because the sailboat requires good strength throughout. Balsa core construction is not needed because there are no large flat areas that need special reinforcing, as in the deck of the cruiser. Of course the preparation of the mold (waxing and buffing) and application of gel coat are the same as for making small boats discussed in Chapter 2, as is the actual work involved in laying up the various layers.

When the two halves are finished, they must be joined. The two molds are pivoted so that they can be bolted together as shown in Figures 4-8 and 4-12. Several layers of matt and roving are worked in along the break, as illustrated in Figures 4-12 through 4-14. These layers make the joint as strong as the sides themselves. The job of putting on these patches is quite unpleasant in the bow and stern where the workers must crawl in the boat under the decks (see Figure 4-12). After the boat is removed from the molds, the outside crack is filled with epoxy filler (see Figure 4-13). It is then ground flush and polished to blend in with the rest of the outside surface (see Figure 4-14). Above the waterline, this joint is carefully finished off with gel coat, wet sanded, buffed with grinding compounds, and polished so that it is no longer visible. An experienced worker will require about 20 hours to complete the seam above the waterline on the two ends of the hull.

It is not necessary to finish the seam as carefully below the waterline, since the seam will not be seen when the boat is in use. However, it must be made smooth. When the bottom is later painted with an antifouling paint, this lower portion of the seam also becomes practically invisible. The portion of the seam along the decks and cabin top is covered up by antiskid material. The seam when finished this way is very rigid and does not open or form cracks after the boat has been in use.

As you have seen so far, there are two methods that can be used to mold a fiberglass boat — the hull-to-deck method used to build a power

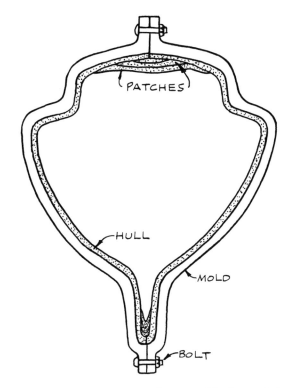

FIGURE 4-8. *Molds for a sailboat bolted together to enable the two halves to be joined. (The two halves have been molded seperately).*

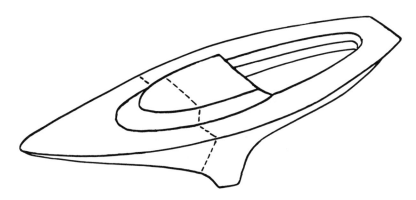

FIGURE 4-9. *The completed sailboat hull. The dotted line indicates the section illustrated in Figure 4-8.*

133

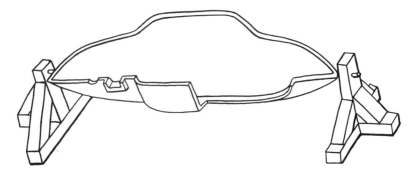

FIGURE 4-10. *Mold for one-half of a sailboat, pivoted into position for easy layup.*

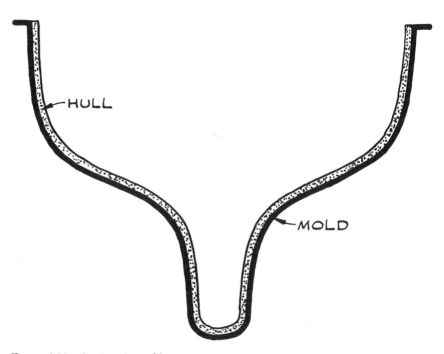

FIGURE 4-11. *Section of a mold.*

134

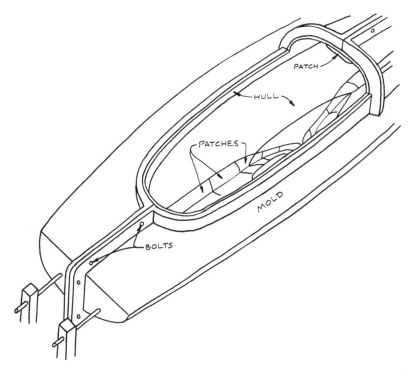

FIGURE 4-12. *Joining the two molds with the two halves of a sailboat together. Note the patches applied along the seam.*

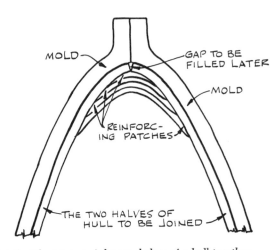

FIGURE 4-13. *Detail of the joining of the two halves of a hull together.*

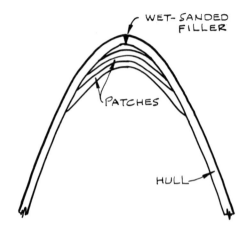

FIGURE 4-14. *Completed joint.*

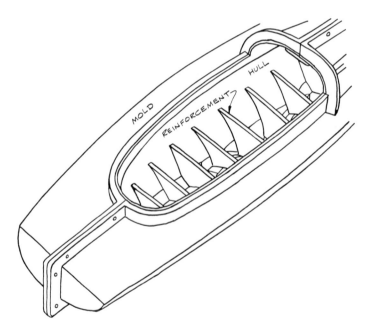

FIGURE 4-15. *Plywood reinforced pieces fiberglassed into the hull with matt and roving patches. The plywood helps tie the two halves of the hull together and provides a mount for the cockpit and cabin flooring as well as the engine and keel bolts.*

136

cruiser, and the split-hull method described above for a sailboat. Both construction techniques can be used to build a sailboat, but which one you choose will depend on the shape of the sailboat involved. Obviously a boat with a flat deck should be assembled like the cruiser, whereas a boat with a sharply crowned deck may be handled advantageously like the sailboat under discussion.

Figure 4-15 shows the boat still in the molds after the two halves have been connected with patches all along the break. Similar to the plywood reinforcement added to the cruiser (Figure 4-3), plywood forms are glassed into the bottom of the hull of the sailboat. They form the framework on which the floor is built, as well as the support for an auxiliary engine. These plywood forms also form a support for the bolts which hold the keel, as shown in Figure 4-16. As you can see in Figure 4-17, the bolts are long and threaded along their entire length. Half of each bolt is embedded in the keel when it is cast; the upper half of the bolt is inserted in a hole through the plywood forms and then through the floor boards, as seen in Figure 4-16. The weight of the keel is transferred from the bolts to the plywood forms which spread the weight over a large portion of the fiberglass hull.

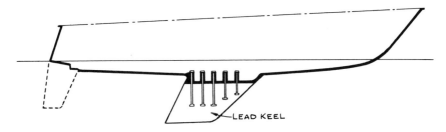

FIGURE 4-16. *Cross-section of a sailboat showing the location of the keel bolts.*

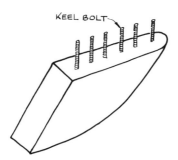

FIGURE 4-17. *A cast keel. The threaded bolts provide a strong bond with lead.*

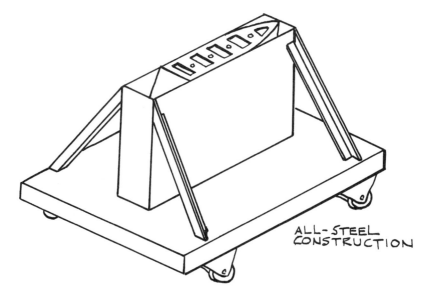

ALL-STEEL
CONSTRUCTION

FIGURE 4-18. *A mold for casting a keel. The keel bolts are inserted in the round holes and the molten lead is poured into the square holes.*

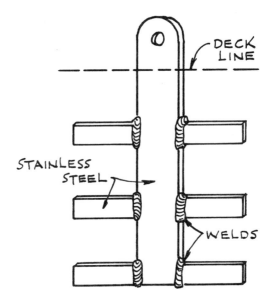

DECK LINE

STAINLESS STEEL

WELDS

FIGURE 4-19. *Chainplate imbedded in the side of a fiberglass sailboat. Only the eye is visible when the boat is completed.*

The keel is made of lead which is melted in a special furnace and poured into a steel mold like the one shown in Figure 4-18. Notice that there are small holes in the top to hold the bolts in place while the lead is being poured and is allowed to harden.

Figure 4-19 shows a good way to make a chainplate, the fitting which holds the metal wires that stay the mast. The arms that are welded onto the shank are secured by the fiberglass, which is molded all around the fittings. Only the upper end with the hole to receive the wire rope sticks out of the deck.

CONCLUSION

As you can see, many of the steps and processes are the same for building large boats as for small ones. The main differences involve the use of balsa core sandwich material, the use of chopped strands for a cheap matt-like layer, and the use of plywood forms to reinforce the bottom of the hull (and to hold the keel and floor). Incidental differences involve the use of a special spray rig, the fact that the workers must walk in the molds to do much of the work, and the large amount of finish work that goes into an expensive yacht.

5/ REPAIRING WITH FIBERGLASS

Fiberglass can be used to make repairs on boats and some household items even though they might not be made of fiberglass. We shall discuss how to make the following repairs:
1. Waterproofing a leaky boat.
2. Repairing a damaged wooden boat.
3. Repairing a damaged fiberglass boat.
4. Repairing a damaged metal boat.

WATERPROOFING A LEAKY BOAT

Fiberglass is very effective for waterproofing a leaky wooden boat. If your boat is planked rather than made of plywood, you will probably want to fiberglass the entire boat rather than just the individual leaky seams.

PLANKED BOATS

Fiberglass applied to wood with polyester resin adheres only moderately well. As discussed in Chapter 1, Vectra polypropylene or Dynel with polyester resin have much higher peel strengths than fiberglass with polyester resin; that is, they are much harder to peel from wood. However, fiberglass has been used many times successfully, and while it might begin to peel more easily, it has superior strength to the other fabrics. The technique for applying each of the various fabrics over wood is basically the same. Vectra polypropylene, however, tends to float in resin. For this reason, only the minimum amount of resin necessary to wet out the fabric should be applied.

To get fiberglass to stick to wood properly, you must prepare the surface carefully. First, turn the boat upside down and completely remove the old finish down to the bare wood. There are various methods for removing old paint — by burning, by using paint removers (solvents), or by sanding. It is not recommended that you remove the old paint by burning, because the oils of the paint may be driven into the wood and will later prevent a good bond between the resin and wood.

The best (although most laborious) method of removing the old finish is to sand it off. If you sand the paint off with a belt sander, you must be very careful not to cut ridges in the wood with the edge of the belt, or to leave uneven spots, both of which are quite easy to do when using a powerful sander with rough paper. It is best to use a paper which seems too fine for the job, as it may surprise you when the power of the belt sander is behind it.

However you do it, the final surface must be smooth, although not glossy smooth. It should have a slight surface roughness which will help the fiberglass to stick.

Second, round all sharp edges to a generous radius (½″ or ¾″ or more). This will help you apply the fiberglass without forming air bubbles. Naturally, if you can not do this for some good reason, you will be able to apply the fiberglass anyway, but the task will be more difficult and probably you will have more air bubbles at the edges.

Third, paint the bare wood with sufficient coats of activated resin to completely fill the grain. The first coat is best thinned with styrene (about five percent by volume) to make it thin so it will soak into the wood. If you are using resin with wax added, you will have to sand between coats unless successive coats are applied before earlier ones set up hard. The final surface should be sanded until it is reasonably smooth (especially be certain there are no runs).

Fourth, place the cloth over the boat, smoothing it out and cutting slits where necessary. Be careful to fold any cut edges you have made in such a way that they will not pull away if something hits them while the boat is being used.

Because you probably will be anxious to save all the weight you can, you will probably want to use only one layer of fiberglass. However, although fiberglass is strong, one layer will probably not be enough to restrain the high cumulative forces exerted by the planking as it expands and contracts. You will need to apply several layers to avoid cracking the fiberglass. The best practice is to alternate matt and cloth. For most boats, one layer of ¾ oz. matt immediately followed by a layer of 10 oz. cloth will suffice. For larger boats, you may need to follow the first matt and cloth layers with the same again.

After thoroughly priming the wood with resin until all pores are sealed, spread the matt and wet it thoroughly. Then before the resin begins to cure, place the cloth on the first layer of matt so it absorbs the

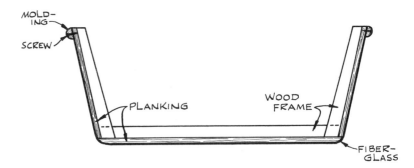

FIGURE 5-1. *Molding applied to the top edge of the planking to keep the edge of the cloth from peeling away.*

excess resin. Use a roller or squeegee to work out air bubbles. Sand off any runs between the first layers of matt and cloth and the next layers of matt and cloth (if used).

After this, follow with enough coats of resin to fill all the pores. This may take two or three additional coats. Wait several days until the resin is no longer tacky, and then paint with an epoxy marine paint for best results. If you use a resin with wax in it for the last coat (so that it will not be tacky), be sure to remove the wax by washing the surface with solvent and sanding it before you attempt to paint.

You should put wood molding (½″ to ¾″, half-round) along the edges where the fiberglass cloth ends at the decks. If you are working on a sailboat to be used for racing, be sure to check your class rules — some classes might forbid the addition of such a molding. This molding, which should extend all around the boat, will protect the edges of the fiberglass cloth from being pulled away when the boat is in use. Also, the molding serves as a rub rail, protecting the paint when alongside docks and other boats. See Figure 5-1 to see how the molding is attached.

PLYWOOD BOATS

If you want to encase the entire hull of a plywood boat in fiberglass, follow the above method, but be careful when rounding the edges as you might cut completely through the thin plywood if you round the edges excessively. Covering the boat entirely in fiberglass might be desirable in a tropical climate where you want to stop marine borers as well as leaks.

You can save weight and materials, however, by just sealing the seams of a plywood boat. Fiberglass cloth is commonly available in large marine supply stores for this purpose, being sold as fiberglass tape. It comes in several widths, the six-inch width being the best one to use.

142

Along each seam to be taped, remove the paint one inch wider on each side of the seam than needed. Round the edges if possible, and sand smooth just as described for the planked boat.

Fill the bare wood with resin, using several coats. Then smooth on the fiberglass tape, wetting it out thoroughly, working out all the air bubbles as you proceed along the length of the tape. Difficulties with air bubbles usually occur more often when using narrow tape on seams than when covering an entire boat with cloth. The tape has a springyness that tends to make it pop up on either side of the edge, and there is not the weight of a larger piece of cloth to restrain it. You must keep brushing the tape as it pops up until the resin gets tacky enough to hold it down. Try to keep air bubbles to a minimum, as they will be the first place to break.

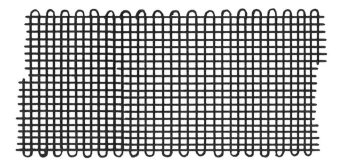

FIGURE 5-2. *The weave of fiberglass tape. The turn of the threads at the edge of the tape makes the edge bulky.*

Unless the air bubbles are really large, you will not want to repair them. But if a bubble extends to the edge of the tape, you will have to repair it. Do so by cutting the bubble away with a sharp knife and then applying a small patch of matt. When the patch has cured, sand lightly to remove the roughness. Be careful not to sand through the cloth.

There will be a noticeable ridge at the two edges of the tape because of the special weaving needed to keep it from unraveling (see Figure 5-2). If you attempt to sand this ridge so that it tapers into the side, sand only about one-half inch in from the edge to avoid weakening the middle portions of the tape. As you sand the edges of the tape into a taper, be careful not to sand hollows in the softer wood next to the tape (see Figures 5-3 and 5-4).

After all this, sand the rest of the paint on the boat until it is smooth; then paint the entire boat with an epoxy marine paint.

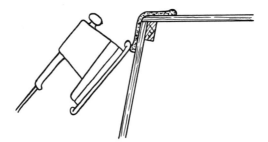

FIGURE 5-3. *Sanding the edge of fiberglass tape, less desirable method. The sander, when held in this position, can easily slip off the tape onto the wood, causing gouges or hollows.*

FIGURE 5-4. *Sanding fiberglass tape, desirable method. The sander is less likely to slip off the tape onto the wood.*

REPAIRING A DAMAGED WOODEN BOAT

There are several ways to use fiberglass to fix a wooden boat that has been damaged. The method you use will depend on the time you can spend on the job — a quick repair for an emergency; a careful, methodical repair if you have all winter to work. It will depend also on your skill, of course, and whether or not you care if someone can tell that the boat has been patched.

EMERGENCY PATCHES

First let us discuss the emergency patch. There are two different situations you might encounter if you rammed something and put a hole in the side of your boat. These are illustrated in Figures 5-5 and 5-6. The less serious situation, shown in Figure 5-6, is where the wood sheathing is ruptured only, and the more serious situation is where a structural frame has been damaged as well.

144

Figures 5-7 and 5-8 illustrate the method used to build up an emergency patch. Notice that the theory of the emergency patch is to apply the patch in such a way that it cannot fall out, even if it has not adhered properly to the wood. This type of patch, of course, looks terrible and should only be used when you must make a patch in a hurry. Its primary disadvantage, other than its appearance, is that it will not add much strength to the damaged area — it is primarily a leak stopper. You cannot depend on it to adhere to the wood for long because this kind of patch is an inflexible mass within a flexing boat. But in an emergency it is better than a big gaping hole! Besides its fast application, the emergency patch has the advantage of not needing many tools — you can carry an emergency repair kit aboard your boat in a small box.

Notice in the accompanying illustrations on emergency patches that you should first bridge the gap with masking tape or something else that will hold up the first layer of cloth until it has hardened. Once the first layer is on, you build on top of it and also fill the hole solidly from the other side. When you apply the masking tape, leave gaps between the

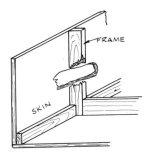

FIGURE 5-5. *Wood boat with skin and frame broken.*

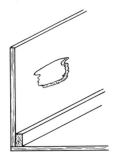

FIGURE 5-6. *Wood boat with skin only broken.*

145

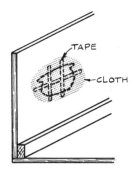

FIGURE 5-7(a). *Wood boat with skin only broken. The inside of an emergency patch is shown.*

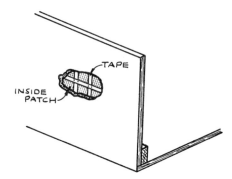

FIGURE 5-7(b). *Outisde of an emergency patch before cloth is applied as on the inside.*

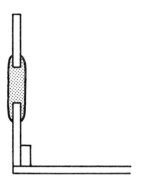

FIGURE 5-7(c). *Cross-section of an emergency patch. The patch will not fall out even if the wood shrinks or flexes.*

146

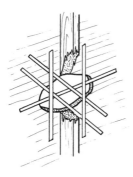

FIGURE 5-8(a). *Wood boat with skin and frame broken. In the first step for making this emergency patch, pieces of masking tape are placed over the hole.*

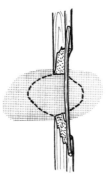

FIGURE 5-8(b). *Fiberglass patch in place over the hole. A twig is then positioned across the top of the broken frame.*

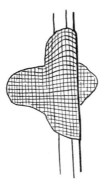

FIGURE 5-8(c). *Fiberglass patch placed over and around the twig and broken frame.*

147

strips of tape so that fiberglass applied from one side of the hole can adhere to fiberglass applied from the other side of the hole. Thus, both sides of the patch adhere to each other and act as one solid mass. The tape remains inside the patch even though it no longer serves its function.

A WOOD PATCH

The patch that most boatbuilders use is shown in Figures 5-9 and 5-10. This type of patch is almost invisible from the outside and looks neat from the inside. You may object that the patch can be seen from the inside, but it is stronger than the invisible patch described later.

This type of patch is essentially a wood patch. Fiberglass is used only to waterproof the repair; you can forget the fiberglass altogether if you fit the wood patch tightly. As you can see in the illustrations, you must cut away enough around the damaged area to get a squared-off shape. This shape is then transferred to another piece of wood that is the same thickness as the original. The resulting patch cut from this piece of wood should fit into the hole fairly tightly. Because the joints between

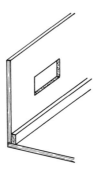

FIGURE 5-9(a). *Making a wood patch. The hole has been squared up.*

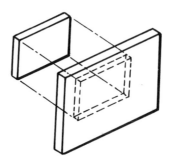

FIGURE 5-9(b). *Making the plug. The inside square must fit the hole perfectly.*

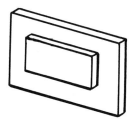

FIGURE 5-9(c). *The finished plug.*

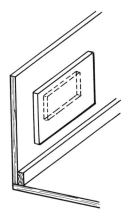

FIGURE 5-9(d). *The plug in place prior to being nailed and glued.*

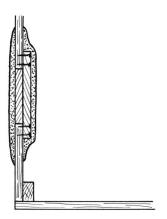

FIGURE 5-9(e). *Cross-section of the finished patch. The plug has been glued, screwed in, and covered with fiberglass cloth.*

149

the original side and the patch are butt joints, the piece that plugs the hole provides little strength. The patch depends on the proper application of glue and a screwed-on backup piece for strength.

If you apply fiberglass cloth to the patch to waterproof it, sand the edges of the fiberglass to a feather edge so that they blend in with the rest of the outside of the boat. Repaint the entire side so the patch will be nearly invisible from the outside.

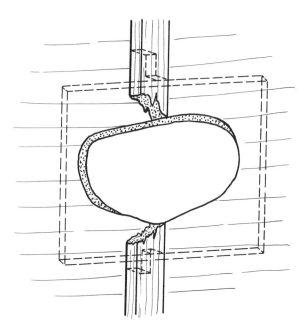

FIGURE 5-10(a). *Wood boat with skin and frame broken. The dotted lines show the areas to be cut away.*

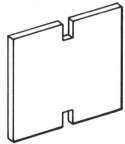

FIGURE 5-10(b). *H-shaped piece to be placed over the hole and around the broken frame.*

150

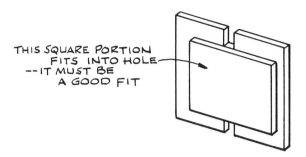

THIS SQUARE PORTION
FITS INTO HOLE
--IT MUST BE
A GOOD FIT

FIGURE 5-10(c). *Square plug attached to the H-shaped piece.*

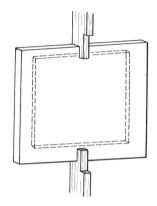

FIGURE 5-10(d). *Patch in place.*

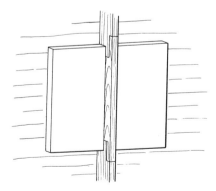

FIGURE 5-10(e). *Frame piece in place. Except for the application of fiberglass, the patch is complete.*

Two different versions of a patch which can be made nearly invisible from both outside and inside are shown in Figures 5-11 and 5-12. The one shown in Figure 5-11 is like the patch described above, but without the backup piece, and therefore it is not as strong. It depends almost entirely on the fiberglass for its strength and is not particularly recommended.

The patch shown in Figure 5-12 is better because some strength can be developed by gluing the tapered edges to the original side of the boat. However, for the glue to hold well, the fit of the patch must be exact, a difficult job for most amateurs. The "sturdy" patch described previously is recommended over either of these patches.

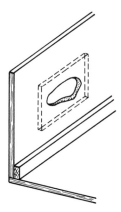

FIGURE 5-11(a). *Another way to patch a wood boat with the skin only broken. The dotted lines indicate the area to be cut away.*

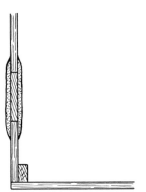

FIGURE 5-11(b). *Wood block glued in and covered with fiberglass cloth on both sides.*

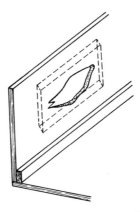

FIGURE 5-12(a). *An invisible patch. The dotted lines indicate the area to be cut away. Notice that the edges are tapered.*

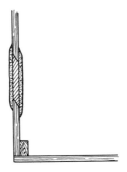

FIGURE 5-12(b). *Cross-section of the completed patch with optional fiberglass cover.*

REPAIRING A DAMAGED FIBERGLASS BOAT

In many instances, fiberglass boats are more complicated to repair than wooden boats, mainly because many areas of fiberglass boats are not accessible from both sides. For emergency patches, however, most of the ideas discussed previously concerning wooden boats also apply to fiberglass boats.

In fiberglass boats, all of the hull and deck and other parts are usually structural to some degree. However some areas such as flanges, rims, edges, and sharply curved areas seem to be critical areas for stresses, so that damage to these areas is more critical than to other areas. For example, damage to the rim around the mast-tube opening in the deck of a sailboard is more critical than damage to a flat area of the deck. In a sailboard, practically none of the inside of the boat is accessible, meaning that all damage must be repaired from the outside only. In other fiberglass boats, both the inside and the outside of a damaged area may be accessible. Therefore, we will discuss the repair of a fiberglass boat from four points of view:

1. Noncritical area accessible from one side only.
2. Noncritical area accessible from both sides.
3. Critical area accessible from one side only.
4. Critical area accessible from both sides.

NONCRITICAL AREA ACCESSIBLE FROM ONE SIDE ONLY

Figure 5-13 illustrates the repair of a damaged noncritical area accessible from only one side, as for example a hole punched in the deck of a sailboard by someone who carelessly dropped the mast on the deck from a considerable height.

After the edges of the hole are smoothed and feathered, as shown in Figure 5-13 (b), the hole is slowly "hemmed in" from all sides until it is considerably smaller than before. This is done by applying small matt patches one or two at a time through the hole on the inside of the damaged area. You must use your fingers to smooth the matt onto the inside of the damaged area so that it bonds firmly. Finally you hem in the hole to the point that you can no longer stick your fingers in with another patch. If you could get inside the hull, the patched area would look somewhat as is shown in Figure 5-13(e).

At this point you begin working from the outside. You add a small patch which covers the remaining small hole as shown in Figure 5-13 (f). Adding more small patches from the outside, as shown in Figure 5-13 (g), you finally work up the surface of the patch until it is almost at the original surface. At this point, fill the remaining area with either gel coat or a filler. If you use gel coat, you will be able to match the original color exactly, but gel coat is very difficult to sand, and you may have trouble getting it to look smooth and unrippled. I recommend that the amateur use an epoxy filler which remains easy to work for an hour or so before turning rock hard. During that hour you have plenty of time to sand it smooth. As you use the sander or sanding block on the epoxy filler, you may find that you still have some hollows which will have to be refilled. When you are done, the filler will harden into a very tough surface which can be painted to match the original gel coat. It should blend in well with the undamaged portion of the boat. Figure 5-13 (h) shows the cross-section of this patch. As you can see, if done well, it should have as much, or more, strength that the area had before being damaged.

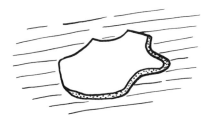

FIGURE 5-13(a). *Patching a hole that is not accessible from one side.*

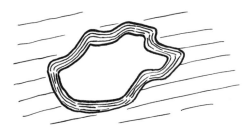

FIGURE 5-13(b). *Edges smoothed and feathered.*

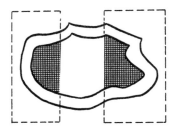

FIGURE 5-13(c). *Supporting patches in place behind the opening.*

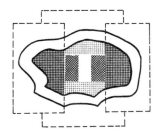

FIGURE 5-13(d). *Six supporting patches in place behind the opening.*

155

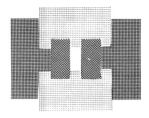

FIGURE 5-13(e). *Back of the hole, showing the overlapping of patches.*

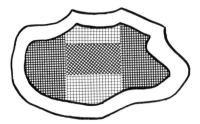

FIGURE 5-13(f). *Patch applied over the opening.*

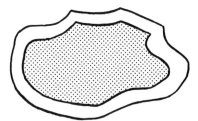

FIGURE 5-13(g). *Final fiberglass patch in place.*

NONCRITICAL AREA ACCESSIBLE FROM BOTH SIDES

Figures 5-14 and 5-15 illustrate the repair of a damaged noncritical area accessible from both sides. Figure 5-14 (b) shows a fairly easy way to patch such an area, which should be adequately strong as long as you allow no air bubbles and clean off the hole thoroughly. The edges are first feathered on the more easily reached side. Then a cardboard with cellophane foil, aluminum foil, or some other parting layer which is smooth and glossy, is placed across the hole on the gel coat side. Filler is placed against the cellophane, and when it is hard, it is backed up with a layer of matt and then several layers of woven cloth.

156

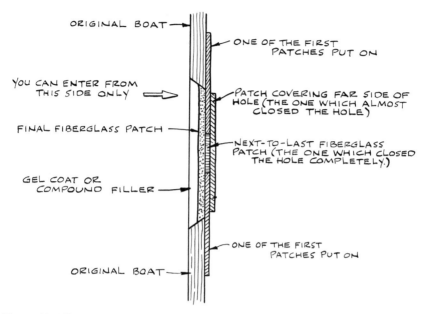

ORIGINAL BOAT →

ONE OF THE FIRST
PATCHES PUT ON

YOU CAN ENTER FROM
THIS SIDE ONLY ⇨

PATCH COVERING FAR SIDE OF
HOLE (THE ONE WHICH ALMOST
CLOSED THE HOLE)

FINAL FIBERGLASS PATCH

NEXT-TO-LAST FIBERGLASS
PATCH (THE ONE WHICH CLOSED
THE HOLE COMPLETELY.)

GEL COAT OR
COMPOUND FILLER →

ONE OF THE FIRST
PATCHES PUT ON

ORIGINAL BOAT →

FIGURE 5-13(h). *Cross-section of the finished patch.*

Figure 5-14 (c) shows a more carefully done patch, such as is recommended by the naval services for the severe conditions their boats must withstand. Here, each layer comprising the original construction is cut away slowly and meticulously to get a stepped effect as shown. Then layers of cloth are inserted, matching those used in the original construction as exactly as possible. This results in a very neat and very strong patch.

This method would be difficult to use if you could not get to the back side, as you need some kind of backing to hold the first layer in place. One way of getting around this problem if you wanted to use this method to repair a hole accessible only from one side would be to insert a piece of hardened cloth which had been formed perfectly flat (or to the appropriate shape). You would have to cut this piece of cloth to exactly the correct shape before inserting it. It is then adhered to the sides of the damaged area with resin and followed with other layers as shown in Figure 5-14 (c).

Figure 5-15 shows a better way to effect the type of patch shown in Figure 5-14 (c). Here you cut away one layer of the original build-up on the less easily reached side, and insert the same kind of cloth into the hole. To get it to lay in at the proper shape, you will have to fabricate a

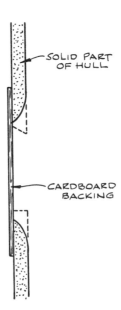

FIGURE 5-14(a). *Hole in fiberglass boat, accessible from both sides.*

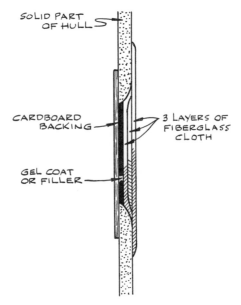

FIGURE 5-14(b). *One method to effect the repair.*

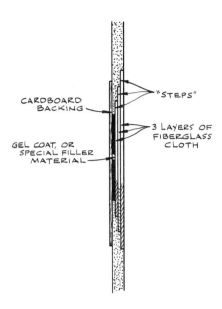

CARDBOARD BACKING

GEL COAT, OR SPECIAL FILLER MATERIAL

"STEPS"

3 LAYERS OF FIBERGLASS CLOTH

FIGURE 5-14(c). *Better method to effect the repair. The area around the hole is "stepped" with a sharp chisel.*

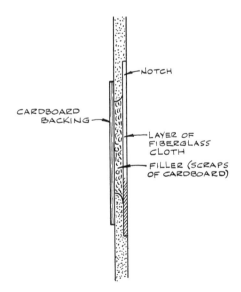

NOTCH

CARDBOARD BACKING

LAYER OF FIBERGLASS CLOTH

FILLER (SCRAPS OF CARDBOARD)

FIGURE 5-15(a). *Better method for repairing a hole in a fiberglass boat, accessible from both sides. The first layer is applied to the less accessible side.*

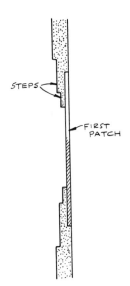

FIGURE 5-15(b). *Cardboard and filler piece removed, steps cut out on the other side. The first patch, when fully cured, will be able to hold the weight of the patches to be added next.*

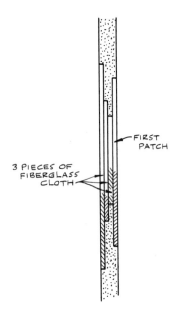

FIGURE 5-15(c). *Finished patch.*

temporary filler, as shown in Figure 5-15 (a), which will later be removed. You will also have to use some kind of parting agent on the filler. After this first layer is on, go to the other side and remove the layers of the original construction in a stepped arrangement as shown in Figure 5-15 (b). Add layers of cloth to finish the patch as shown in Figure 5-15 (c).

CRITICAL AREA ACCESSIBLE FROM ONE SIDE ONLY

Figure 5-16 shows a damaged critical area accessible from one side only. The area shown is the mast-tube opening in the deck of a sailboard. Not only has the deck been damaged, but part of the mast tube also has been damaged, as shown in Figure 5-16 (a). Actually, the mast tube part can be reached from both sides at this point before the deck hole is repaired. Therefore, we will take advantage of this.

The first step in making the repair is to install cardboard back-up pieces as shown in Figure 5-16 (b), with parting agent on the side facing the patch to come. When spreading the parting agent, you must be careful not to get any on the edges of the damaged area, as the patch must adhere to these edges. Since the mast must fit down inside the tube when repaired, you must be careful, when placing the cardboard, to maintain the original diameter.

Fill in the damaged portion of the mast tube with a layer of matt and several layers of woven cloth, as shown in Figure 5-16 (c). Because the edge between these layers of cloth and the undamaged portion of the mast tube is nearly a butt joint, there is not much strength to be gained from this joint. Therefore, you need to add a piece of roving which goes completely around the mast tube as shown in Figure 5-16 (d).

Now that the mast-tube portion of the damage is repaired, the cardboard is removed, and you proceed to repair the adjoining deck. Because the deck portion is only accessible from one side, you have to approach it as you would the repair shown in Figure 5-13. Finish this patch off just like the one described in Figure 5-13.

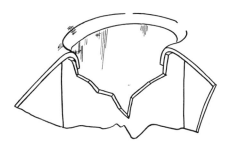

Figure 5-16(a). *Damaged mast tube and deck.*

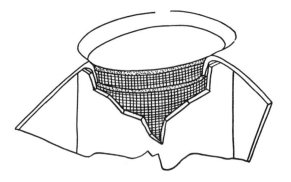

FIGURE 5-16(b). *Cardboard in place to maintain the critical diameters.*

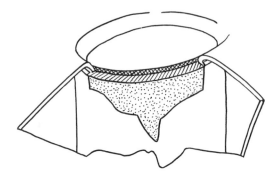

FIGURE 5-16(c). *Hole in mast tube filled in with several layers of matt and cloth.*

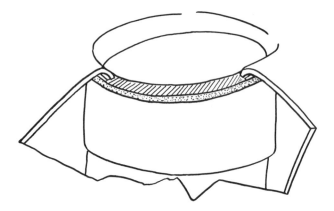

FIGURE 5-16(d). *Mast tube reinforced with roving all around.*

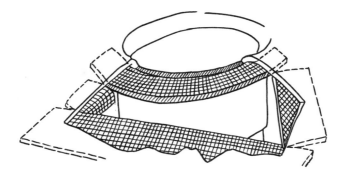

FIGURE 5-16(e). *Proceeding with the repair of the deck area.*

CRITICAL AREA ACCESSIBLE FROM BOTH SIDES

Figure 5-17 illustrates a damaged critical area completely accessible from both sides. The method used to repair this damage utilizes "steps" obtained by cutting layer after layer of the original construction as illustrated in Figure 5-14. The repair is started by cutting the steps as shown in Figure 5-17 (b), then by placing cardboard in back of each patch-to-be as in Figure 5-17 (c). Then the layers are built up as shown in Figure 5-17 (d and e). As you can see, the sharply curved area where the projection meets the flat deck presents some difficulties. The best way to handle it is to leave it until last and then fill it with filler as shown by the dotted lines of Figure 5-17 (d). If the inside appearance of this curve must be maintained, the repair may be very difficult — you will have to fashion a cardboard backing to take the exact shape of the curve before laying down your first layer of cloth. It has been assumed in this patch

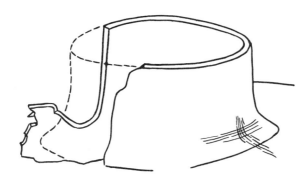

FIGURE 5-17(a). *Damaged mast opening.*

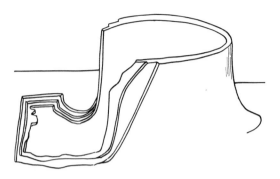

FIGURE 5-17(b). *Edges prepared for patches. The original layers of fiberglass have been removed in steps.*

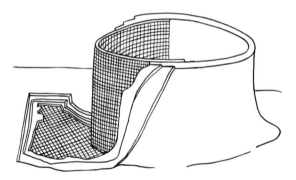

FIGURE 5-17(c). *Cardboard backing in place to maintain critical dimension.*

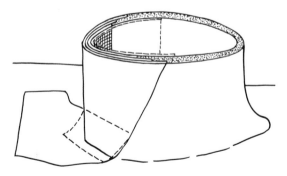

FIGURE 5-17(d). *Patch almost completed. The rounded junction between the mast opening and the deck, shown by dotted lines, must be added.*

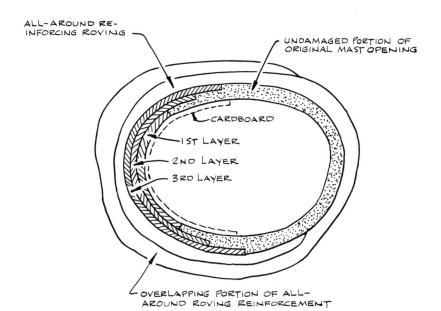

ALL-AROUND RE-
INFORCING ROVING

UNDAMAGED PORTION OF
ORIGINAL MAST OPENING

CARDBOARD

1ST LAYER

2ND LAYER

3RD LAYER

OVERLAPPING PORTION OF ALL-
AROUND ROVING REINFORCEMENT

FIGURE 5-17(e). *Cross-section of mast opening repair.*

that the inside dimensions had to be maintained (as if a mast fit into the opening). Therefore, to obtain added strength, the outside dimensions were altered somewhat by adding a piece of roving completely around the circular projection.

Using these examples you should be able to figure out how to fix almost any damage you encounter in your boat.

REPAIRING BROKEN-OUT AIR BUBBLES

As explained in Chapter 3, even the most carefully built fiberglass boat is liable to have a few air bubbles that might escape detection. These bubbles might break open later when the boat is in use. Generally these broken air bubbles will not be bigger than a nickel in size. The outer gel coat will chip off, revealing the matt or cloth underneath, which will have a textured look and a dark green color from the resin.

To fix this type of blemish you will have to roughen the surface of the cloth somewhat by scratching it. Now follow with a small amount of gel coat of the same color as the original, sanding it with wet sandpaper until it blends into the original. Then buff the patch with grinding compounds to restore the gloss and finish with fiberglass polish. Or you may prefer to fill the blemish with an epoxy filler, which will be easier to sand smooth. This must be followed with paint matching the original gel coat.

Occasionally, you will encounter a broken air bubble that is much bigger than the size of a nickel; in fact you might be confronted with a large void. In this case you must roughen the surface of the cloth and fill the hole with small pieces of fiberglass matt or cloth, finishing with gel coat or filler and paint as described above. Or you may prefer to fill the entire void with epoxy filler; however, this method is not as good as filling the void with numerous pieces of cloth put in carefully one at a time.

REPAIRING A DAMAGED METAL BOAT

Fiberglass is effective for making an emergency repair for a metal boat. The same methods used on wooden boats apply to metal boats. Fiberglass and polyester resin, however, are not recommended for the permanent repair of metal boats. The best way to repair a metal boat is to weld or rivet patches in place.

If epoxy resin is used rather than polyester resin, often a good patch can be made for a metal boat. The techniques to be used are similar to those used for repairing wooden and fiberglass boats.

CONCLUSION

Since repair services are very expensive, by effecting your own repairs, you should be able to save a considerable amount of money. It is reputed that the big money is in the fiberglass repair business rather than in the fiberglass boat-building business — do your own repairs and save money.

APPENDIX A
OTHER METHODS OF MAKING FIBERGLASS BOATS

There are various ways of making fiberglass boats other than the hand-layup process using a cavity mold — the method described in detail in this book. The hand-layup process is the one used by most small- and large-boat manufacturers, and it results in a fine product. However, there are methods, such as matched-die molding, which can give as good or better results more consistently and with less dependence on the integrity of the labor force. Since these methods involve higher initial set-up costs, they are not widely used, and are definitely prohibitive in cost for large fiberglass boats.

There are also fiberglass construction methods that are inferior in sophistication and result in inferior products unless extreme care is taken. The problem is relative, though. Hand-layup is not foolproof; the methods that I am now going to discuss are, in my opinion, much less foolproof. It is easier to make a poor boat with these methods, although the best job can be equal in quality to one turned out by the hand-layup process.

These alternate, less foolproof methods are what you might call "one-shot" methods; that is, they are intended to provide one, and only one, finished boat per set-up. They are intended to put one-boat fiberglass construction in the same cost bracket as one-boat wooden construction.

The cost of building a separate mold is the part of hand-layup fiberglass construction that makes building a fiberglass boat from scratch as expensive as buying a finished boat retail. Many alternate methods get around this by making the mold an integral part of the finished boat. The mold contributes to the strength of the hull as long as the boat lasts. Other alternate methods favor the building of a very cheap and fragile mold that will not cost much but will last long enough to build one boat. Something similar to this could be done using the plaster and screening method suggested for building a plug in Chapter 3. Many of these methods are discussed in *Fiberglass Boats You Can Build*, published by Motor Boating.

LIGHTWEIGHT WOODEN BOAT METHOD

An unusual fiberglass construction method involves building a lightweight version of the finished boat out of wood. The wood and the method of fastening it are not, in themselves, strong enough to make a serviceable boat. As the boat is constructed, however, all joints are filled with matt and resin instead of glue before they are screwed together. The same applies to the planking put over the frames. With this method, joints do not have to be made carefully because the matt and resin will fill them. After finishing the boat, all surfaces, including frames, are covered with matt and then cloth. These layers, which cover both the outside and the inside of the boat, touch the matt squeezed out of the joints, bonding the entire boat together. The result is a fiberglass boat with a wood interior throughout, similar to the balsa core construction used to build certain parts of large fiberglass boats as discussed in Chapter 4. Figure A-1 shows a cross section through a frame of a boat built by this method.

There is no reason why these methods and others like them cannot produce a satisfactory boat. It should be obvious that they would not be satisfactory for more than one boat, but they probably could save you considerable money on a one-shot building project. However, you may experience some problems. For instance, the cheap-mold process may be much more difficult than it looks. You have to spread paper over the

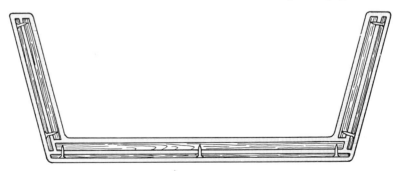

FIGURE A-1. *Cross-section of a lightweight wooden boat covered with fiberglass and resin.*

frames without wrinkling it and then, after the plaster is applied, sand smooth a concave curve without punching a hole in it. The lightweight wooden boat method may result in a lumpy boat from matt that has squeezed out between the joints, unless you are willing to engage in careful sanding before putting on the final layers. However, all methods, even including the hand-layup method discussed in Chapter 2, involve problems, so it may be that you will be able to use these alternative methods successfully.

BUILDING A BOAT USING HEAT-FORMABLE FOAM

Heat-formable foam construction combines elements of both the cheap-mold and lightweight wood mold methods described previously. First a lightweight frame is built. This frame is covered with a plastic drop-cloth, which is stapled on in order to prevent resin from sticking to the mold. Next, pieces of foam are stapled to the mold and covered with fiberglass. When sufficient layers of fiberglass have been put on, the foam and fiberglass shell is removed from the mold, and the inside of the hull is covered with layers of fiberglass cloth. The result is a sandwich-type construction with fiberglass on the outside and foam on the inside. This type of construction results in a strong, lightweight boat that requires a minimum of building materials. In addition, the foam provides positive flotation for the hull.

That is the general picture. Now for some details. The frames are erected on a 2″ x 8″ base that is on wheels so it can be moved out of your garage. The entire mold on wheels takes about six hours to build. The ¼″ foam is stapled on the mold with ½″ staples. Although the foam will bend easily to most of the curves, compound curves require cutting and heating (with heat lamps) to make the foam fit. Though difficult to learn at first, this cutting and heating soon becomes a fast process. The entire hull can be covered in four hours. The keel does not use the foam. Instead, it is a solid layup which is done in sheets on a smooth surface (such as masonite). After installation, it is cut to its final shape.

Pulling the foam, which has been glassed over on one side, from the mold may be difficult because of the staples used to hold the foam to the mold. If the foam cannot be worked loose, the entire works may have to be turned over and the mold pulled out of the shell piece by piece. The wood should be pulled out in big pieces, though, because it can be used again in later stages of construction. Several areas must be reinforced with extra foam and roving before the bare hull is complete. When both sides of the foam are covered with fiberglass, the resin seeps through the cracks between the pieces of foam, helping to bond the entire assembly together.

This kind of construction can result in a good-looking and strong boat if you are careful about fitting the foam to the mold, and if you do not injure the foam when pulling it free of the mold just prior to glassing the inside. If you are not able to get a good fit with the foam, you may have a very rough job.

CONCLUSION

These and other methods all attempt to get around the problems and high cost of making a mold, such as that used in hand-lay-up. Although they are not as foolproof as hand-layup, they can result in good boats if the builder is very careful.

APPENDIX B
USE OF PAPER AND FOIL IN HANDLING WET FIBERGLASS

Chapters 1 and 2 gave you some hints on how to handle wet fiberglass cloth and matt, but primarily you were told and shown only how they should look when you are done, leaving you to your own devices to get them that way. The reason for this is that descriptions in a book on how to handle wetted-out fiberglass are almost worthless; words and illustrations cannot adequately show the necessary movements you must use. There are, however, a few shortcuts you can use to make your learning experiences easier.

Specifically, let us discuss the emergency patch shown in Figure 5-8 of Chapter 5. In that illustration the broken member is shown in a vertical position. The broken area has been spanned by a twig. You are told to drape strips of matt over the twig to either side of the broken frame. The first step would be to lay a strip of matt on a flat surface, wet it out with resin quickly but thoroughly, and then, carefully picking it up and holding each end of the strip, drape it over the twig and pat the ends against the side of the boat until the strip sticks. If the weight of the cloth pulls the matt away as soon as you remove your hand, try again with a narrower strip. Several such thin strips will be needed to build up a framework along the entire length of the patch. When you get the strips to stick, leave them alone until the resin cures.

Continue to build the patch up with more pieces of matt until the layer is solid. Follow with roving until the patch is built up to sufficient strength. The first few strips are hardest to get to stay in place. Once these are hardened, the next ones will be held up by these first ones, making them relatively easy to put on.

Now look at the alternate method of handling the same repair shown in Figures B-1 through B-3. Here a stiff piece of paper (or light card-

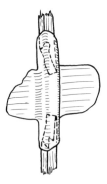

FIGURE B-1. *Using a paper form to bridge the gap of a broken frame.*

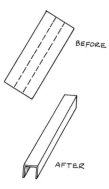

FIGURE B-2. *Paper before and after folding.*

board) has been cut and bent to present a smooth, filled-in form instead of the twig. Not only will the resulting patch look better using this paper form, but the strips of fiberglass will stick easier to the paper than to the twig. This is because part of the strip of fiberglass will not be hanging unsupported in the space between the twig and the side of the hole. The paper which is enclosed inside the patch will not hurt anything if it is made just big enough to cover the hole, and will not keep any parts of the patch from touching and bonding together.

This idea of using paper and foil may help you with various problems. One amateur who found matt difficult to handle solved his problem by putting the matt on a piece of aluminum foil. After wetting the piece of matt on the foil, which was lying on his workbench, he picked it up on the foil side and pressed the matt side against the area needing the matt. Pressing the foil gently and evenly to get it to stick, he then peeled the

PAPER FORM

FIGURE B-3. *Cross-section of a repair done with a paper form.*

foil away, leaving a glossy, smooth surface on the matt patch. Although the smooth surface would not be desirable for the reinforcing patches discussed in Chapter 2, it might be useful for some repair work where the patch is to be the outermost layer. If you want a slightly roughened surface, you could brush it gently, being very careful not to overdo it.

Use paper and foil wherever you can, especially while you are still learning. And when using a paper form, always plan it so that when buried inside the patch, the paper will not prevent all parts of the patch that must bond together from doing so.

BIBLIOGRAPHY

BOOKS FOR FURTHER STUDY

*Arkhangelskii, Boris A., and Alshits, I. M., *Plastic Boatbuilding*, New York: Pergamon Press, 1964, $4.50.

*Bell, Charles, *How to Build Fiberglass Boats*, New York: Coward-McCann, 1957, $6.50.

†Brewer, Edward S., and Betts, Jim, *Understanding Boat Design*, Camden, Maine: International Marine Publishing Co., 1971, $4.95.

†Chapelle, Howard I., *Yacht Designing and Planning*, New York: W. W. Norton, 1936, 1964, $15.00.

*Chapman, Charles F., *Fiberglass Boats You Can Build*, New York: Motor Boating, $5.00.

*Chapman, Charles F., and Horenburger, Frederick W., *Practical Boat Building*, New York: Motor Boating, $5.00.

†Cobb, Boughton, Jr., *Fiberglass Boats: Construction and Maintenance*, New York: Yachting, 1969, $4.95.

Designs for 363 Boats You Can Build, New York: Motor Boating, 1965, $3.00.

*Out of print; locate in used book store or library.
†Available through the publisher of this book, International Marine Publishing Co., Camden, Maine.

*Du Plessis, Hugo, *Fiberglass Boats: Fitting Out, Maintenance, and Repair*, Tuckahoe, N.Y.: John de Graff, 1964, $12.50.

†Gardner, John, *The Use of Plastics in Boatbuilding*, Camden, Maine: International Marine Publishing Co., $3.00.

Gibbs & Cox, Inc., *Marine Design Manual for Fiberglass Reinforced Plastic*, New York: McGraw-Hill, 1960, $19.50.

Gibbs & Cox, Inc., *Marine Survey Manual for Fiberglass Reinforced Plastics*, Tuckahoe, N.Y.: John de Graff, 1962, $15.00.

†Kinney, Francis S., *Skene's Elements of Yacht Design*, New York: Dodd, Mead, 1962, $15.00.

Penn, W. S., *GRP Technology: Handbook to the Polyester Fiberplastics Industry*, Levittown, N.Y.: Transatlantic Arts, $20.00.

Safety Standards for Small Craft, American Boat and Yacht Council, 1971, $10.00.

Sonneborn, Ralph H., et. al., *Fiberglass Reinforced Plastics*, New York: Rheinhold, $8.00.

LISTS OF SUPPLIERS

The Thomas Publishing Company (461 Eighth Ave., New York, N.Y. 10001) is the publisher of many catalogs giving sources of supply. The *Thomas Register*, at $30.00 postpaid, lists all manufacturers in the United States by product and state in six volumes.

Retailers and distributors are not listed unless they sell to other manufacturers. Manufacturers of "end" products, i.e., those sold to the consumer, are not usually listed. This is a very good reference for suppliers of fiberglass cloth and resins in your area, giving the address and capital worth of each company. The seventh volume has two sections: one lists all companies alphabetically, and the other gives trademark information. Thomas Publishing also carries smaller catalogs with more specialized listings; write for more information.

INDEX

Note: page numbers in italic type refer to illustrations.

177